WHAT IS PHILOSOPHY?

An Introduction

Alistair J. Sinclair Ph.D.

DUNEDIN

Published by
Dunedin Academic Press Ltd
Hudson House
8 Albany Street
Edinburgh EH1 3QB
Scotland

ISBN 978-1-903765-94-4

British Library Cataloguing in Publication Data
A catalogue record for this book is available from the British Library

Typeset by Makar Publishing Production

Printed in Great Britain by Cromwell Press

O vitae philosophia dux, o virtutis indagatrix expultrixque vitiorum!

O philosophy, guide of life, explorer of the good in us, and expeller of the evil in us!

Cicero, Tusculan Disputations (44 <small>BCE</small>), V, 5

Contents

Introduction

What philosophy is about

What is philosophy? In a sense, we all can answer that question, as philosophy is meant for everyone. We may make of it as little or as much as we please. But the more we make of philosophy, the more seriously we must take it. This book is for those who want to take a serious look at philosophy without necessarily becoming serious philosophers. It will particularly interest young people and adults who want to understand the basics of philosophy and get a gist of what the well-known philosophers were saying. It provides an overview which will hopefully give beginners the confidence to take their study of philosophy further. They may discover areas of special interest to them, be inspired to read the works of the great philosophers, or to consult, for instance, online resources such as the Stanford Encyclopedia of Philosophy and Wikipedia without being bemused by the choice and range of material available.

Philosophy ought to appeal to all of us because it comes from our sense of wonder about the universe and our place in it. As a species, we are naturally curious about everything, and we desire to know and understand things. As individuals, we want to be wise rather than plain ignorant. Hence the word 'philosophy' means 'love of wisdom' in Greek. It originally covered all intellectual pursuits. Everyone earnestly seeking knowledge and understanding was called a philosopher.

Whenever we think deeply and consistently about our ideas, concepts, principles, theories, morals, or ways of living, we are doing philosophy. How do we know what we know? What is it to be a good person? What is art? Is an electron a real or imaginary object? Is religion fantasy or reality? These are all philosophical questions, and in considering them, we are philosophers of some type or other: see 'Types of Philosopher', below.

Every human activity has its 'philosophy'. We can have a philosophy of how to run a business, of playing golf, shopping, eating carefully, or whatever. Our thinking about an activity becomes a philosophy when we think seriously about it and have our reasons for doing what we do. We philosophise about it when we examine what it involves and how it relates to other activities similar to or different from it.

Philosophy is therefore the ultimate thinking activity. It reflects what is most distinctive about us as a species, namely, our ability to think abstractly about things. Once we humans give up thinking and questioning everything, we are indeed a doomed species. Any attempt to narrow its scope threatens our freedom to think about things from new, different and unaccustomed perspectives. But that is the general view of philosophy. There is also the academic study of philosophy which has developed in western culture as a distinct subject.

How philosophy works

Philosophy is basically what philosophers do and there is no method peculiar to it. There are as many definitions of philosophy as there are philosophers willing to formulate them. Philosophy as a whole is best understood by studying what the various important philosophers have made of it down the ages. If we take philosophy seriously, we need to understand how philosophy developed as a distinct discipline and how other disciplines began as philosophical pursuits and eventually arrived at their own methods and ways of studying their subject matter.

Outstanding philosophers usually rethink their ideas at a very simple level and then build up a complex system of thought from simple elements. Their philosophies are peculiar to themselves as they reflect their individuality. When such philosophers attract public attention they may become fashion-setters as far as ideas and attitudes are concerned. They impress the public with the strength of their ideas, but whether these ideas are ultimately true is another matter.

As a result, elementary philosophy books may not introduce philosophy in the way that introductory books in physics, chemistry or economics do. Any so-called introduction to philosophy contains one philosopher's particular and peculiar view of philosophy, including this one. Unlike introductions to the sciences which are of limited interest to experts, the expert philosopher always puts forward his own view of philosophy in such introductions. But his philosophy will not be important unless he works out his peculiar point of view to the extent that the great philosophers did. Thus, great philosophers such as Kant, Russell, Heidegger and Sartre wrote introductions which outlined their own views as much as 'introduced' philosophy as such.

Philosophy works only when particular philosophers interest and enthuse the general public with their writings and lectures. This is usually because their respective philosophies are persuasive, illuminating and even inspiring. Without public recognition, the works of philosophers may only achieve a cult status. It is arguable that creating a profession out of philosophy has progressively marginalised it as professional philosophers are more interested in pleasing each other than the public at large.

The study of philosophy

Philosophy applies to us all in so far as we all have a philosophy of life of some sort. Even if we live for shopping or for football, these are philosophies of life. But the study of philosophy involves much more. It involves examining the different points of view, world views, or perspectives which philosophers have used to understand ourselves and our place in the universe. *Studying* philosophy is therefore distinct from *having* a philosophy. We can have a philosophy even though we haven't thought about it very deeply. We may call ourselves philosophers, in spite of not having studied philosophy as a subject. But what sort of philosophers are we? John Macmurray did not think much of this unexpressed philosophy:

> It is all very well to say that every man and every society of men has its own philosophy. That is only true in a most unhelpful sense. It might be truer to say that their philosophy holds them in its grip and tosses them about helplessly from one surprise to another. The trouble is that very few men and fewer societies have any clear idea what their philosophy is. It remains unexpressed and half-conscious, implicit in their ways of behaviour, in their hopes and fears, in their ambitions and rivalry. The task of the philosopher is to turn the searchlight of deliberate thinking upon this heaving darkness. It is to express in coherent meaningful terms what is usually only implicit in the way we live. It is this effort that draws the boundary line between practice and theory, between understanding life and living it. Nor can the effort to understand fail to make a difference in life itself . . . When we understand, though not till then, we are in a position to control, to plan and to change.[1]

It follows from the above that philosophy differs from religion in being based on understanding rather than on belief. People who depend on their beliefs alone are not being philosophers unless they try to understand what their beliefs are all about at a philosophical level. Philosophy is always looking for the answers whereas a religion already has all its answers. Thus, Bertrand Russell argues that the value of philosophy lies in its very uncertainty:

> The man who has no tincture of philosophy goes through life imprisoned in the prejudices derived from common sense, from the habitual beliefs of his age or his nation, and from convictions which have grown up in his mind without the co-operation or consent of

his deliberate reason. To such a man the world tends to become definite, finite, obvious; common objects rouse no questions, and unfamiliar possibilities are contemptuously rejected. As soon as we begin to philosophise, on the contrary, we find that even the most everyday things lead to problems to which only very incomplete answers can be given. Philosophy, though unable to tell us with certainty what is the true answer to the doubts which it raises, is able to suggest many possibilities which enlarge our thoughts and free them from the tyranny of custom.[2.]

Russell's rather sceptical view of the role of philosophy is typical, as we shall see, of the empiricist outlook. The rationalist outlook is more optimistic about the possibilities of our reasoning powers. Whatever view we take, philosophy is very much what we want to make of it, and our philosophising expresses of our freedom of thought. We are thinking for ourselves alone, even though we inevitably go through the same thought processes that philosophers in the past have already gone through. In fact, all sorts of people can become philosophers.

Types of philosopher

Oral philosophers

We are all philosophers of some kind, depending on our ability and our commitment to the subject. We all can voice our respective philosophies of life. But we are no more than oral philosophers if we have never worked out our philosophy critically nor studied philosophy as a subject. We can recognise the philosopher within us and benefit from philosophising at our own level. Indeed, we need to get people arguing about philosophy in general to generate public interest in it. Joseph Addison recognised that when he wrote in *The Spectator* (1711):

> I shall be ambitious to have it said of me that I have brought Philosophy out of the Closets and Libraries, Schools and Colleges, to dwell in Clubs and Assemblies, at Tea-Tables and in Coffee-Houses.[3]

Street philosophers

They are the pseudo-intellectuals and know-alls who pretend to have more knowledge and wisdom than they really possess. They regale people with half-canned theories, ill thought out solutions to everything, conspiracy theories and the like. William Hazlitt wrote an interesting essay called 'On People With One Idea' (1824) in which he describes those street philosophers only interested in talking about one thing. The most extreme example of a street philosopher is Charles Dickens' schoolmaster character Mr Wackford Squeers in *Nicholas Nickleby*, who says the following:

Philosophy's the chap for me. If a parent asks a question in the classical, commercial, or mathematical line, says I, gravely, 'Why, sir, in the first place, are you a philosopher?' 'No, Mr. Squeers,' he says, 'I an't.' 'Then Sir,' says I, 'I am sorry for you, for I shan't be able to explain it.' Naturally, the parent goes away and wishes he was a philosopher, and, equally naturally, thinks I'm one.[4]

Amateur philosophers

They have studied philosophy principally for their own enjoyment. And they have often studied enough philosophy to be well aware of their own ignorance of the subject. The best of them are the equal of Socrates, while the worst of them are no more than street philosophers.

Student philosophers

They are studying philosophy in a formal way at school, college or university. They are not necessarily any better for their studies. Unless they learn to use their knowledge in positive and practical ways, they may never become true philosophers.

Academic philosophers

They are qualified in philosophy at degree level though they are not earning their living by being philosophers. Whether they are any use as philosophers may be questionable. It depends perhaps on whether they can use their respective philosophies to benefit other people besides themselves.

Professional philosophers

They earn their living by teaching and researching into philosophy or by writing books, appearing on television and so on. They may have brilliant minds and know the core of philosophy through and through but that does not make them great philosophers.

Literary philosophers

They are those famous writers who had ideas but did not produce systems of philosophy. Their achievements were more literary than philosophical. They played around with philosophical ideas in a literary or poetical way that is insightful but not rigorous or consistent. They include essayists such as Michel de Montaigne, Thomas Carlyle and Ralph Waldo Emerson, and playwrights such as George Bernard Shaw.

Aphoristic philosophers

They are those thinkers who only expressed their ideas in short paragraphs or 'aphorisms'. They lacked the ability, concentration or inclination to develop their thinking systematically and critically. They include Nietzsche and Wittgenstein who, however, have become so notorious that they are generally though mistakenly classified as 'great philosophers'.

Great philosophers

They are systematic philosophers who have thought out their ideas to a more profound level than most philosophers. But they are great also because of the influence that they have had on subsequent generations of philosophers. Nearly all of them are long dead. But this need not deter any of us from striving to be great philosophers.

//

Why are there no great women philosophers?

This question is strictly a subject for psychological research, but the following reasons are possible, whatever their ultimate merits:

◈ In the past, their achievements may have been ignored or attributed to male philosophers.

◈ Male thinking is strategic and global whereas female thinking is tactical and detailed. Therefore philosophical thinking is more of male than a female preoccupation because it requires us to look at things from an all-encompassing point of view.

◈ Women tend to be more sociable and more interested in people than in abstract ideas as compared with men.

◈ The construction of a systematic philosophy demands undivided attention and concentration which perhaps suits the obsessive nature of men more than the more balanced thinking of women.

Philosophy is one of the ways by which men can assert their manhood in a relatively sociable and harmless way. It is therefore arguable that we should encourage men more than women to challenge and assert themselves through this medium. This book reflects this argument, while recognising the vital role that women can make to the subject.

\\

Be a true philosopher!

We can't all be great philosophers, but we can at least aspire to be true philosophers. We alone know when we are being true philosophers, whether people call us such or not. We can all seek the truth in our own way by trying to get to the bottom of things. There is great joy to be gained in having fresh insights and making novel connections between things. True philosophers are always moving on and are never content with reaching an end to their thinking. They are never certain that they or anyone else has reached the ultimate truth of the

How to be a great philosopher

The great philosophers distinguished themselves by making significant contributions to knowledge and understanding. They thought differently from their contemporaries and they changed people's minds and ways of thinking about things. The world is therefore different in specific ways as a result of the changes they brought about. In their quest for truth, they improved our knowledge and understanding about ourselves and our place in the universe. Also their greatness was ensured because they benefited from at least some of the following attributes:

◈ **Their talents:** They were persons of immense talent and ability who worked out their respective philosophies to a far greater degree than the rest of us.

◈ **Their insights:** They offered comprehensive philosophies that give us profound insights which are still relevant to our understanding of the human condition today.

◈ **Their diligence:** They were diligent in studying the works of their predecessors so that they could effectively stand on the shoulders of giants to offer us something new and important. They were also diligent and persistent in working out their ideas in detail and in presenting them to the public.

◈ **Their environment:** They flourished in an intellectual atmosphere that encouraged philosophical thinking and rewarded innovative thinking instead of repressing or ignoring it. They discussed their thoughts and ideas with other people within public places, schools, clubs, societies or universities.

◈ **Their fashionableness:** Their philosophies were of great interest to the public and it became fashionable to read their writings and discuss them. They were therefore fortunate in living during periods when philosophy was in vogue and widely read and discussed by the public.

◈ **Their influence:** They had immense influence on successive generations of thinkers whose thinking developed and changed by studying their works.

◈ **Their shortcomings:** Their greatness meant also that they acknowledged their shortcomings and laboured to overcome them. Being mere human beings, even the greatest of philosophers were not privy to the whole truth of things. It was for their successors to better their predecessors and not to pretend that they were infallible. Many of the great philosophers were let down by their successors who made too much of their works instead of correcting them and moving beyond them. This applies for example to Plato and Aristotle, whose works became the subject of blind adoration instead of insightful criticism.

matter. Persuasive arguments are not accepted just because they are persuasive. Indeed, they are considered suspicious because they are persuasive.

True philosophers don't tell people *what* to think but *how* to think. They want to improve their own and other people's thinking as they want to think more accurately about how things are in reality. They are more interested in teaching and being taught rather than in preaching and being preached to. They want to

The benefits of philosophy

The serious study of philosophy may confer the following benefits (by no means guaranteed):

Intellectual benefits

◈ It develops critical thinking.
◈ It improves the ability to analyse problems dispassionately.
◈ It enables us to see how ideas have shaped the world down the centuries.

Social benefits

◈ It helps us to be more communicative persons.
◈ We see the advantage of having different perspectives and points of view.
◈ We are better able to understand the workings of society and our role in them.

Personal benefits

◈ Philosophy can cleanse the soul of negativity by making sense of what seems senseless.
◈ It helps us to find our place in the universe by enabling us to see ourselves in context.
◈ It can be an enjoyable way of using our brains by playing with ideas.
◈ It is the highest form of pleasure since it involves one's whole personality.
◈ By lifting our thoughts on high, it is the ultimate heavenly pursuit.

empower people rather than wield power over them. No one is meant to believe everything that the philosopher is telling them; they are meant to work it out for themselves. Those philosophers who compel absolute and uncritical belief in their views are not being true to the spirit of philosophy. Such dogmatists have figured all too frequently in the history of philosophy and sadly some are still regarded today as being 'great philosophers'.

Yet true philosophers don't go to the other extreme and become sceptical of all beliefs and opinions. They may believe most fervently in this or that, but they hold their beliefs at arm's length. They are prepared to rethink them at any time. As we shall see, taking a balanced, middle way between the extremes of scepticism and dogmatism is essential for fruitful philosophising.

True philosophers keep an even keel in being true to themselves, other people, the facts, and their past and their future. This constant self-reference leads to increasing self-knowledge, the end of which is to know one's place in the universe and be suitably humbled by it. Philosophy thus helps us to accept our position stoically and we can experience great joy and contentment in working for a better world, even in the humblest way.

We can better the world in a humble way by sticking to our principles within the framework of a philosophy which is always open to criticism and further development. Principles by themselves are not enough. Principles such as 'trust no one', 'always tell the truth', 'better mind my own business', 'live and let live', may be subject to exceptions and we need our philosophy to help us make these exceptions. Otherwise, our principles become dogmas that enslave us rather than serve us. If I see someone being beaten up, I may excuse myself for doing nothing by thinking 'Ah well, better mind my own business.' But I would find it difficult to live with myself if the person died and I could have done something to prevent it. Thus, the true philosopher is a principled person who is also open-minded and uses their judgment with flexibility.

Learning the core of philosophy

Academic philosophy since the nineteenth century has been increasingly pro-fessionalised around a core of history, subjects and problems. The study of phil-osophy therefore involves studying this core even though new movements in philosophy may originate outside philosophy. Philosophical movements may result from changes and advances outside this core and in, for example, science, economics or politics. But these movements will not be well founded or per-suasive in the long term unless they refer to the core of philosophy and take account of philosophy as a whole. The arguments of this book suggest that philosophy has been prematurely professionalised and that it is too narrowly defined around this core.

The core history of philosophy

This comprises those western philosophers who are generally accepted to be 'great philosophers' and who have made distinctive contributions to human thought. Only a selected number of these philosophers are profiled in this book.

The core subjects of philosophy

The following subjects form the core of most philosophy courses:
Metaphysics – What is reality? Mind and matter. Language and reference.
Epistemology – What is knowledge? How do you know that you know?

Ontology – What is existence? What kinds of things exist?

Logic – What is a valid argument? The laws of thought.

Ethics – What is a good person? Values and facts. Why should you behave yourself?

Aesthetics – What is art? *chacun à son goût* (each to their own taste)

The core problems of philosophy

These problems include personal identity, causation, freewill and determinism, induction, the reality or unreality of time, the nature of truth and *a priori* knowledge. One of the biggest problems in philosophy is the apparently irreconcilable distinction between empiricism and rationalism. The need to reconcile these opposing points of view is argued for strongly in this book.

The peripheral subjects of philosophy

Professional philosophers also contribute to subjects on the boundary of philosophy. These include political philosophy, the philosophy of psychology and the philosophy of science. They are peripheral to philosophy only in the sense that distinct sciences now deal with their respective subject matters.

The omnicompetence of philosophy

When philosophy has been disparaged, periods of intellectual stagnation have ensued during which society loses its sense of direction. In other words, the role of philosophy in society is analogous to that of a conductor of an orchestra. Without a conductor or lead musician, an orchestra slowly loses its harmony and descends into a cacophony. Without a coherent philosophy to keep it on track, a society similarly descends very slowly into chaos and anarchy. The more complex and developed the society, the slower its decline, but without philosophy, it will surely lose its way, sooner or later. The history of philosophy, as outlined in this book, is evidence of the powerful effect that philosophy has always had on western culture, leading to the eventual dominance of that culture in the world.

Just as every person has a philosophy, so every academic subject has a philosophical basis. There are philosophies of science, religion, economics and so on. Whenever we think critically about the ideas, concepts and theories of any academic subject, we are doing philosophy. Whenever questions arise about abstract and speculative matters, we use philosophy to answer these questions. There is no way of clearly distinguishing philosophy as an academic subject from the philosophising that enters into the study of all academic subjects.

Philosophy at its best is a trial-and-error process of getting at the truth through persistent probing and self-criticism. Science gives us a particularly rigorous way of doing this by experimenting, researching, investigating the nature of things, and offering rigorous theories with mathematical or conceptual precision. But philosophy rather than science contributes to the advancement of scientific knowledge as a whole. It alone can stand outside all the sciences and see them as a whole by means of imaginative speculation. In other words, new sciences and new ways of ordering knowledge are produced by speculative philosophers rather than by scientists operating within current scientific methods or paradigms.

Philosophy rather than science is 'omnicompetent' and capable of giving us those answers that our reasoning powers can give us, however adequate or inadequate these answers may prove to be. The various sciences give answers only within their current methodologies or what Kuhn calls 'normal science' which is only amended by radical changes in opinion or 'paradigm shifts' as he calls them.[5] Such shifts require new philosophical thinking rather than an extension of current scientific thinking. For example:

➲ When scientists provide answers outwith the current sciences, they do so as philosophers and not as scientists. Einstein behaved as a philosopher when he stood outside the given theories of physics and saw them from a completely different perspective which gave rise to the special and general theories of relativity.

➲ The thinking of scientists is often stimulated by ideas and concepts that have little or nothing to do with the scientific problems they are dealing with. For example, Charles Darwin and Alfred Russell Wallace had both read Malthus's *Essay on Population*[6] and they used the philosophical implications of that work to complete the theory of evolution, arrived at independently by them.

➲ In his eloquent book, *Physics and Philosophy* (1962), the Nobel prize physicist Werner Heisenberg shows how the new physics differs from classical physics in its use of philosophical concepts. He discusses the difficulties of using current language and logic to encompass 'the mathematical scheme of quantum theory'.[7] He implies that progress in understanding the latter theory is a philosophical rather than a scientific matter.

Thus, speculation about scientific theories usually consists in a philosophical examination and criticism of existing ideas and concepts. It introduces new or revised ideas and concepts within a new theoretical framework. The end-product becomes a purely scientific matter only when it is given conceptual or mathematical precision, and is developed into a systematic theory amenable to experiment, observation or other trial-and-error procedures required to verify or falsify the theory.

However, philosophy's omnicompetence has often been marred by its failings, particularly when philosophers go to extremes and take their ideas to their logical conclusion. Philosophy in general helps us to order our abstract thinking about things. But we can go too far in one direction or another and end up in the extremes of dogmatism or scepticism, empiricism or rationalism and, more recently, reductionism or holism. Such 'isms', among others, have often prevented philosophy from being as beneficial to humanity as it might have been. The outline of philosophical history in this book shows how often philosophy has ground to a halt when it encounters such philosophical log-jams in our thinking. Nineteenth-century idealism is an example of such an impasse. This book attempts to show how philosophy has developed in spite of these extremes and where its future may lie.

The dynamic nature of philosophy

Philosophy at its best is a dynamic process that is ever moving and never stable. It is dynamic in the original sense of the Greek word *dunamis* which refers to the 'power' or 'potential' in things. That is to say, philosophy elicits the potential within our ideas. It is concerned less with what these ideas actually are than with their potential, by which we make more of them than they are at the moment. In other words, philosophy is productive only in moving forward to a better understanding of things rather than resting with things as they are at the moment.

Paradoxically, philosophy moves forward by being *recursive* or backward-looking. It looks back at what has been said or written and sees more in it than what was originally intended. It moves on by bringing forth the meanings of statements which have been already made. Such 'strange loops' are a fundamental part of our thinking, as Hofstadter points out in books such as *Gödel, Escher, Bach* (1980).[8] They confound the view that logic and mathematics are sufficient to explain human reasoning.

Recursive thinking enables us to interact meaningfully with ideas, concepts and problems by stepping outside them. We don't get emotionally involved with them but treat them dispassionately. We are intrigued by them without becoming partisan or overconfident of them. Our belief in their value is based on sound reasons and not just on emotional commitment or respect for authority.

Philosophy can never rest on its laurels as it is ever poised on a knife-edge between knowledge and belief. Science may provide us with lasting knowledge, and religion may give us fixed belief. But philosophy seeks the truth underlying all knowledge and belief. But, as already mentioned, philosophers lapse all too easily into either dogmatism or scepticism. The more they believe in the truths they arrives at, the more dogmatic and overconfident they may become. The more they examine any body of knowledge, the more elusive they may find truth to be and they become sceptical and disillusioned as a result.

The dynamism that keeps philosophy going involves both metaphysical speculation and logical analysis. Speculation is basically intuitive. It means grasping things as a whole and all at once. An idea, a thought, a hypothesis, a theory, or even a complete system of philosophy may emerge from such abstract, metaphysical speculation. But logical analysis is required to unpack the idea, theory or system and make sense of their contents. It completes the recursive loop mentioned above.

While speculation is rationalist and idealist, logical analysis is empiricist and realist. The first incorporates everything into one thing, while the second multiplies distinctions without end. Speculation by itself generates dogmatic overconfidence in its conclusions while analysis by itself leads to sceptical uncertainty about everything. A dynamic philosophy is essentially dualistic as it moves from speculation to analysis and vice versa. The oscillation between the two prevents ossification and stagnation. Through critical analysis of successive intuitions we gain greater insights and move towards truth. Scientific theorising often follows this procedure.

While the great philosophers have always been passionately committed to their respective philosophies, they have usually worked hard to clarify their views though both speculation and analysis. When they cease to move forward in critically developing their philosophy, they have often lapsed into dogmatic adherence to their views or sceptical dismissal of them. Popper is perhaps an example of a philosopher who became dogmatically committed to his views, and Hume, for example, became sceptical of the value of his own philosophy since, apart from theology, he wrote no more on philosophy in the last twenty years of his life.

The great philosophers considered in this book are chosen because they exemplify the way that philosophy has changed and moved on. Other philosophers have made important contributions to the movement of philosophy but the ones chosen here also show how philosophy is prone to the extremes of dogmatism and scepticism.

Philosophy makes progress by constantly clarifying the problems facing humanity. When lasting solutions are arrived at, these become sciences or areas of study in their right. They are marginalised to the periphery of philosophy. They continue to generate philosophical problems but these are usually specific to the particular science or area of study.

Philosophy is the perennial activity by which we constantly examine ourselves and our role in the universe. If we give up thinking about our plight and what we can do about it, we are truly done for. The history of philosophy shows that periods of the greatest human achievement coincide with periods of fruitful philosophical activity. The Renaissance and the Enlightenment were periods of widespread cultural and economic achievement whereas the unphilosophical Dark Ages period was relatively stagnant and unproductive. We therefore need philosophy to give us confidence in ourselves and our future.

Philosophy and science

Historically, scientists thought of themselves as 'philosophers' till the nineteenth century. Darwin was called 'the philosopher' by the crew of the *Beagle*,[9] and even Glasgow engineers and technologists in the early nineteenth century regarded themselves as 'philosophers'.[10] The word 'scientist' was only coined in 1833 at a British Association meeting in Cambridge when Coleridge objected that 'philosopher' was 'too wide and lofty a term' and William Whewell suggested 'scientist' in its place.[11] Whewell clearly saw scientists as being cataloguers and experimenters while he himself remained an aloof philosopher. All the sciences of the nineteenth century emerged from philosophy at their inception. And their further development depends as much on their philosophical as on their scientific or experimental achievements.

In recent years, some eminent scientists have forsaken their disciplines to produce philosophical works of varying degrees of competence. Beginning with Paul Davies' seminal work, *God and the New Physics* (1983),[12] this trend has culminated in Richard Dawkins' ill-advised polemic, *The God Delusion* (2006). Dawkins aims to promote atheism and supersede religion but his philosophical naivety undermines the anti-religious cause. He weakens his case by demonstrating the cultural necessity of religion and by making a metaphysical use of 'memes' that are purportedly the cultural analogue of 'genes'.[13] His arguments suggest that we will never get rid of religion. Instead, he advocates a competing religion of his own which is a kind of biological scientism. He believes that the four main roles of religion: 'explanation, exhortation, consolation and inspiration' can be fulfilled by science which is enough of a religion for us all.[14] But he is merely introducing yet another religion into a crowded marketplace, instead of getting rid of it. If religion is as bad as he makes it out to be, then he should propose an alternative to it that goes beyond all existing religions to make it unnecessary for anyone to believe absolutely in anything based on authoritarian imposition, divine scripture, superstition or the supernatural.[15] But he is philosophically incapable of seeing an alternative to science and religion that belongs to neither of them.

The more assiduously that scientists defend science against all comers, the more their beliefs become indistinguishable from religious beliefs. Their beliefs become 'scientism' which is a philosophy instead of science. As is argued above, scientists will only advance our knowledge and understanding significantly by becoming competent philosophers themselves. When the scientist ventures into philosophy, 'he is a brother metaphysician with a rival theory of first principles', as F.H. Bradley put it.[16] He is concerned with the metaphysics which elucidate the underlying principles behind the physical reality portrayed in the scientific view of things. Paul Davies in his latest book, *The Goldilocks Enigma* (2006), shows the extent to which speculation in physics is becoming metaphysical rather scientific.[17] A new subject is emerging which might be called *metaphysical cosmology*. This trend is evident in works such as those by David Deutsch, *The Fabric of Reality* (1997), Lee Smolin, *The Life of the Cosmos* (1997) and Amit Goswani, *The Self-Aware Universe* (1995). In these works, physicists are becoming metaphysical in their attempts to make sense of the universe and our place in it. It appears inevitable that metaphysics will come to the fore while scientists await the next theoretical advances in their respective disciplines.

Philosophy as a western phenomenon

The great philosophers were all western philosophers because philosophy developed as a distinct subject in ancient Greek culture. The word 'philosophy' was popularised by Pythagoras but it was Plato who delineated the role of the philosopher and distinguished it from the role of the sophist. In his view, the philosopher, unlike the sophist, did not simply teach young men to be clever orators who manipulated the populace for their own ends. The philosopher pursued knowledge for its own sake. In particular, he sought to understand the nature of the forms of things as is argued in Plato's great but flawed dialogue, *The Republic.*

Philosophy is essentially a western phenomenon because of the individualistic nature of the great philosophers. Each of them is one of a kind. Eastern thinkers in contrast tended to be more imbedded in the prevailing religion and culture in which they lived. They were more like cult figures than individualists obstinately ploughing their own fields.

Moreover, classical Greek philosophy in particular applied reason to the material world in a way that is not found in the speculative systems of India, the mysticism of Taoism, or the gentlemanly precepts of Confucianism. The ancient Greeks believed that reason was an essential feature of human beings and not just the prerogative of philosophers. It was fashionable among the Greeks to be lovers of truth who were possessed with a passion for knowledge of all kinds.[18] Otherwise, they would have had no lasting interest in philosophers or their offerings. Such a singlemindedness in the pursuit of philosophy has been a particular characteristic of western culture. It was not found anywhere else in the world until recent times.

Philosophy was the making of our civilisation. It made the difference that ensured the eventual triumph of western culture over other world cultures. The history of philosophy shows us how the West came to dominate the rest of the world through the power of its ideas. The interactive and argumentative nature of philosophy helped westerners, as individuals, to keep their wits together to a greater extent than the rest of world. By clear thinking, they were better placed to exploit any opportunities that life had to offer. Perhaps they were too efficient in doing so, to the point of criminal exploitation. The pursuit of individuality can bring out the worst in people as well as the best, and the role of the greatest philosophers has always been to moderate these excesses by giving us increasingly accurate insights into our nature.

This book is unashamedly about western philosophy and western philosophers. Now that our culture has been adopted in various forms throughout the world, philosophy in the twenty-first century will doubtless no longer be confined to any particular part of the world.

Notes

1. John Macmurray (1936), *Interpreting the Universe*, New York: Humanity Books, 1996, pp. 2–3.
2. Bertrand Russell (1912), *The Problems of Philosophy*, London: Oxford University Press, 1970, ch. 15, p. 91.
3. Joseph Addison, (1711), *The Spectator*, Vol. I, London: J.M. Dent, 1909, no. 10, Monday, 12 March, 1711, p. 39.
4. Charles Dickens (1839), *Nicholas Nickelby*, London: Collins, 1967, ch. 57, p. 696.
5. Thomas S. Kuhn (1970), *The Structure of Scientific Revolutions*, Chicago: University of Chicago Press, 1970, ch. III, p. 24 and ch. VII, p. 66.
6. Cf. Thomas Robert Malthus (1803), *An Essay on the Principle of Population*, Harmondsworth: Penguin, 1979, in the Introduction by Anthony Flew, pp. 49–51.
7. Werner Heisenberg (1962), *Physics and Philosophy*, London: Penguin, 2000, ch. 10, p. 124.
8. Douglas R. Hofstadter, (1979), *Gödel, Escher, Bach: An Eternal Golden Braid*, Harmondsworth: Penguin, 1980. Also, with Daniel C. Dennett (1981), *Mind's I*, Harmondsworth: Penguin, 1986. In his latest book, *I am a Strange Loop*, New York: Basic Books, 2007, Hofstadter deals with the 'strange loop' philosophically, but sadly (cf. p. xvii) he doesn't consider himself to be enough of a philosopher to get to the bottom of it.
9. Charles Darwin (1833), *The Correspondence of Charles Darwin*, Vol. I, 1821–1836, ed. Frederick Burkhardt and Sydney Smith, Cambridge: Cambridge University Press, 1985, p. 313. To Miss Catherine Darwin, Maldonado. Rio Plata, 22nd May to 14th July 1833: 'Was ever a Philosopher (my standard name on board) placed between two such bundles of Hay?'
10. Cf. Minute Book of the Glasgow Philosophical Society from November 1802 to August 1820. Glasgow University Archives, DC 118/2/1. This society is still extant as the Royal Philosophical Society of Glasgow. See its website at: www.royalphil.org.
11. Cf. Nigel Leask (1998), in a Queen's College, Cambridge website, 'Coleridge and the Idea of University': www.queens.cam.ac.uk/Queens/Record/1998/Academic/coleridge.html:
    It is a little known fact that Coleridge was responsible for the coining of the term 'scientist' by his disciple William Whewell at the British Association's meeting in Cambridge in June 1833. Coleridge objected at the meeting that 'philosopher' was 'too wide and lofty a term' for those underlabourers who collocated facts under conceptions, and Whewell accordingly suggested the term 'scientist', a category which he would not, however, have been happy to apply to himself as a gentleman mathematician and higher philosophical manager of the sciences.
    The British Association for the Advancement of Science was founded in York in 1831 and is still going strong. See its website at: www.the-ba.net.
12. Paul Davies (1983), *God and the New Physics*, Harmondsworth: Penguin, 1984. Davies acknowledges (p. viii) that this is not 'a science book' but 'a book *about* science'. As he freely uses works of philosophy in his discussions, he is indulging in philosophy though he is coy about saying so.
13. Richard Dawkins (2006), *The God Delusion*, London: Transworld Publishers, 2007, ch. 10, pp. 222–34, esp. p. 231.
14. Ibid., ch. 10, p. 389, and pp. 404–5.
15. For my own inadequate attempts at suggesting alternatives to religion, see my book: *The Answers Lie Within Us*, Aldershot: Ashgate, 1998, and a recent online article: 'A Humanist's Faith: Towards a Humanist Alternative to Religion', in *Essays on the Philosophy of Humanism*, available at www.essaysinhumanism.org/07sinclair.pdf
16. F.H. Bradley (1897), *Appearance and Reality*, Oxford: Oxford University Press, 1969, Introduction, p. 1.
17. Paul Davies (2006), *The Goldilocks Enigma*, London: Penguin, 2007. See especially the last chapter, ch. 10, 'How Come 'Existence?', p. 251.
18. Cf. Plato, *The Republic*, trans. D. Lee, Harmondsworth: Penguin, 1974, Book Five, 475b–476, p. 268.

PART 1

The Development of Philosophy

1.1 Early Greek Philosophy

> The first men who insisted upon 'speaking in terms of nature,' as Aristotle
> says, are certain wise men of Ionia who were legislators and merchant
> princes in their own seafaring republics precariously perched on the rim
> of Asia Minor in very much the same way as the early North American
> settlements were perched on the rim of our continent. They were the
> Jeffersons and Franklins of their time.
>
> Giorgio de Santillana, *The Origins of Scientific Thought* (1961)[1]

Humanity made a huge stride forward during the 500s BCE when the early Greeks
discovered abstract, objective thinking and exploited it to the full. For the first
time, people recognised the significance of abstract words such as nature, truth,
time and justice. They no longer regarded such words as being magical, divine
or demonic but as things they could use to make sense of the world for themselves. Nature, for instance, was no longer to be feared or worshipped but to be
understood. This is the story of how this stupendous intellectual development
came about by the invention of philosophy as we now know it.

//

Why philosophy arose among the Greeks

Unique features of Greek culture such as the following ensured that philosophy arose
among them and no other ancient people:

The nature of Greek religion

Philosophy developed independently of religion because Greek religion was not based on
a fixed system of doctrines and was not rigidly enforced by an élite organisation of priests.
In Greek culture, there was as much emphasis on trade, industry and money-making as
on religious observance. This was largely because Greece was not agriculturally rich and it
depended on trade and industry for its prosperity. Trade brought them into contact with
religions and cultures alien to theirs. Thus, criticism of religion was tolerated up to a point
since the Greeks welcomed discussion about religious matters.

The dominance of the poets

Greek mythology was restated and elaborated by poets and playwrights. Homer and Hesiod and other poets, as well as the playwrights such as Aeschylus, Sophocles and Euripides, made their own interpretations of the Greek myths and stories. The early philosophers carried on that tradition by publishing their works in a poetical form. The Greek public was receptive to their works because their minds were open to new ways of thinking.

The political nature of the oracle system

The Delphic oracle in particular was an important arbiter between the city states and was consulted also as regards their internal affairs. Thus, religion served the needs and aims of city states rather than vice versa, as in Egypt, where the principal cities were built for the purposes of religion. Oracular pronouncements were often obscure and ambiguous but they always made sense to those who used them. This promoted a rational approach to problems and led to genuine attempts to find the best way of dealing with them, instead of relying on nothing but prayers, appeals, sacrifices, libations to the gods, examination of entrails and the like.

The individuality of the city states

The cities competed with each other and largely avoided war by their treaties, ties, sport, and their shared Greekness. Each state was a living experiment in which they sought the best way to govern and organise their citizens. This also made them open to new ideas and new ways of thinking which they used to improve their cities and increase their reputation among the Greeks.

The practicality of the early sages and philosophers

The early philosophers engaged in politics, organised engineering schemes, and used their astronomical and geometrical knowledge for practical purposes. This practical bent made them keen to get to the bottom of things and find out what really made things as they are. Thus, there was no distinction in their minds between speculation and practical pursuits, as we shall see was the case with the earliest of the Greek philosophers.

The Ionian physicists

The first philosophers in the sense of being those who loved wisdom, truth and knowledge for their own sake, were the Ionian physicists. They were called 'physicists' because they were concerned with the 'physis' or nature of things. They were the first men to put religious thoughts out of their heads and wonder about what the world was really made of. Instead of thinking of everything in terms of gods, spirits, demons and the like, they thought of the world as being made of matter of some sort. They began to think abstractly and objectively about the world by using concepts to understand the world rather than attributing everything to the divine thoughts and actions outside their control.

The Ionian physicists were Thales, Anaximander and Anaximenes who lived in Miletus, an Ionian Greek city situated on the west coast of Turkey south of present-day Kuşadasi and opposite the island of Samos. In its day, it was a very prosperous manufacturing and trading port. Its textile goods were famous throughout the Greek-speaking area. Its trade and industry made it a cosmopolitan city which was open to new ideas and new ways of thinking. It therefore fostered and encouraged the speculative thinking which led to philosophy as we now know it.

Thales (c.623–c.545 BCE)

Thales of Miletus was the first man in history who looked at the world in a material and non-religious way. He no longer saw material objects as being made of nothing but spirits or demons. He concluded that material objects must be made of a primary substance or *archê* and he thought that substance must be water. He observed what was happening in nature and he saw that water is needed to germinate seeds, to give birth, and to keep us alive. Water seemed to him to condense out of the air in the form of rain. It can also be boiled back into air in the form of steam. Solid objects like stones may be melted down into fluid glass or molten metal. These must have appeared to him to be forms of condensed water. Therefore it made sense to him that everything can either be condensed into water or rarefied out of water. His conclusions may seem simplistic to us, but this was a major breakthrough in our thinking that set us on the path to science and technology. Nowadays, we follow Thales's way of thinking when we think of things as being ultimately reducible to energy.

Though Thales was the first speculative thinker of this type, he was renowned in his own time as a politician, engineer and inventor. He was fully involved in the affairs of his city, and in the war against the Persians he used his engineering skills to divert a river and make it fordable for the troops. He predicted the eclipse of the sun in 585 BCE. When he was ridiculed for his poverty, he responded by buying up all the olive presses out of season and renting them out when they were in demand. But he did this only to show how easy it is to make money. He was thus the first recorded businessman as well as the first of the speculative thinkers.

Anaximander (c.610–c.546 BCE)

Anaximander of Miletus was a student and successor to Thales but he took speculation in an even more abstract direction. He disagreed with his mentor as he questioned whether everything could be explained in terms of a material substance like water. There are dry things as well as wet things and they are in opposition to each other. Also, cold things are opposed to warm things. They can't be both warm and cold at the same time. He therefore concluded that the everchanging dividing line between these opposites was fundamental to nature. He called this dividing line the 'indefinite' (*apeiron*) and called it the primary substance. In this startling leap of human thought, he used a metaphysical term for the first time to account for the workings of the material world. Furthermore, he speculated that the opposites were at war with each other and destroy each other. They come into being and pass away, 'for they pay penalty and retribution to each other for their injustice according to the assessment of time'.[2] In this single statement, quoted from his book, Anaximander accounts for the death and destruction of life and matter. Everything comes out of the indefinite substance and returns to it eventually because their existence is an injustice to other things which is paid for in the course of time. In other words, life is a kind of tribunal in which we are judged according to our deserts and how well we have used the time allotted to us. This is a precursor of the religious ideas developed by Plato in the Myth of Er in his dialogue, *The Republic*.

Anaximander's speculations concerning the origins of life were even more audacious. He thought that the first living creatures originated in moisture and that they were each encased in a prickly bark from which they emerged on dry land. It was obvious to him human beings must have originated from another species because we cannot survive unsupported like other species. Originally, we were nurtured inside fish-like creatures and emerged able to look after ourselves. He clearly had a vague inkling of what we now call the theory of evolution. Unfortunately, men's minds were not yet ready to prove or disprove such speculations by looking at the evidence in an orderly and systematic way. His speculations therefore remained a mere curiosity to succeeding generations.

Yet Anaximander was not a remote armchair speculator. He drew the first map of the known world showing shorelines and oceans. He probably did so to aid Miletian trade in the Black Sea and Mediterranean. He seems to have been more famous in Miletus for his political and practical activities than for his speculations, as recent excavations at the site of Miletus have uncovered part of a statue with his name on it. This indicates his importance as a civic figure rather than as the great philosopher he is now considered to be.

Anaximenes (c.590–c.525 BCE)

Anaximenes of Miletus was a student of Anaximander, but he continued the tradition of speculating for himself about how things are made up. He agreed with his mentor that the primary substance is one and infinite but he disagreed that it is completely indeterminate. Everything must be reducible to some definite kind of matter. He observed that air is unseen and untouchable, and he concluded it is indefinite enough to be that from which everything is either condensed or rarefied. Air is evenly distributed everywhere until it subjected to heating which turns it into fire. When it is cooled it is condensed first into mist or cloud, then into water, and finally into solid matter such as earth or stones. It seemed to him that hotness and dryness rarefy things, whereas coldness and wetness are condensed. Again, as with Anaximander, such clever speculations were not checked with how nature actually works. They were the subject of teaching within an exclusive school rather than the objects of empirical research within a scientific community.

Although the school of Anaximenes survived the Persian takeover of Miletus in 546 BCE, it seems to have ossified thereafter. It produced no more independent thinkers of the same stature, even after the death of Anaximenes. This was possibly because his successors formed an inward-looking clique to defend themselves against an increasing intolerance of free speculation. The school was eventually wiped out in 494 BCE when Miletus was razed to the ground. The pre-eminence of Miletus among the Greeks came to an end and thereafter the mantle of philosophy and literature passed to Athens. Carl Sagan speculates in *Cosmos* (1981) that if Ionia had not come under the yoke of the Persians, the scientific advances later made by Newton and Einstein might have been made a thousand years sooner, provided that Ionian philosophy had continued to develop.[3] However, this view is questionable if the pursuit of philosophy had already become dogmatic, inverted and devoid of dynamism.

The early dogmatic thinkers

The first philosophers were practical men fully involved in the affairs of their respective cities. But their thinking was only practical up to a point. They were not the open-minded, self-critical thinkers that we expect scientists to be nowadays. Their thinking remained essentially dogmatic. They worked out in their heads what they believed the truth to be and then asserted it to be so beyond doubt. The most important of the early dogmatic thinkers was Pythagoras.

When Ionia was taken over by the Persians in 546 BCE, they imposed governors on the Ionian cities. The atmosphere became more oppressive and there was less tolerance of freethinking philosophers. Many chose to leave and travel to other Greek-speaking regions. These include Pythagoras and Heracleitus.

Pythagoras (c.570–c.500 BCE)

The name of Pythagoras outshines that of any other early Greek philosopher, and rightly so since the whole science of mathematics originates in his work and that of his successors. He was reputedly born on Samos and his interest in mathematics may have been stimulated by early visits to Babylonia and Egypt, but scholarly opinion is divided on that matter. Certainly he brought to the study of mathematics something of an oriental adoration. Numbers were not just the ultimate objects of reality for him they were also the subject of worship and mystical contemplation. He drew attention to the geometrical nature of numbers, hence 'square numbers'. Some scholars argue that the so-called Hindu-Arabic figures – 1, 2, 3 etc. – were originally invented by Neo-Pythagorean scholars from a geometrical joining of dots. These figures were taken to Persia and India in the sixth century CE after the philosophical schools were closed in the Christian west.

According this view, the zero originates from the first letter of the Greek *ouden* meaning 'nothing'.[4]

It is difficult to distinguish Pythagoras' teachings from those of his disciples. None of his writings has survived, and Pythagoreans invariably supported their doctrines by indiscriminately citing their master's authority. Pythagoras, however, is generally credited with the theory of the functional significance of numbers in the objective world and in music. In other words, he recognised the theoretical usefulness of numbers and how they are used harmonically in music. Other discoveries often attributed to him (e.g. the incommensurability of the side and diagonal of a square, and the Pythagorean theorem for right angle triangles) were probably developed only later by the Pythagorean school. More probably the bulk of the intellectual tradition originating with Pythagoras himself belongs to mystical wisdom rather than to scientific discovery. The principles of Pythagoreanism, including belief in the immortality and reincarnation of the soul and in the liberating power of abstinence and asceticism, influenced the thought of Plato and Aristotle and contributed to the development of mathematics and western rational philosophy. The proportions of musical intervals and scales were first studied by Pythagoras, and he was the first influential western practitioner of vegetarianism.

Heracleitus (c.540–c.480 BCE)

Heracleitus of Ephesus is one of the best known and most influential of the Presocratic philosophers (the philosophers before Socrates). His book was considered profound and obscure. Socrates allegedly said that it would take a Delian diver to get to the bottom of it.[5] Nevertheless his theory is coherent enough to make some sense to us.. Indeed, he was the first thinker to think of his theory as being objective and as applying to everything in common. This is the meaning of the opening statement of his book called 'Of Nature':

> Of the Word (*logos*) as I describe it, men always prove to be uncomprehending, both before they have heard it and after they have heard it. For although all things happen according to this Word, men are like people with no experience, even when they experience such words and deeds as I explain, and when I distinguish each thing according to its constitution and show how it is. Other men do not notice what they do when they are awake, just as they forget what they do when asleep.[6]

Heracleitus is here referring to people's inability to objectify their account of the world (their 'Word') and treat it as something distinct from their immediate experience of things around them. It is as if they were sleepwalking through their lives because they cannot comprehend the deeper meaning underlying their lives.

Thus, wisdom for Heracleitus was not knowledge of many things but an ability to see the underlying unity between interacting opposites. 'It is a harmony of opposing tensions, like that of the bow and the lyre.' Health is balanced by its opposite which is ill-health. Thus, changes in one direction are balanced by changes in the other direction. For example, health and disease define each other. Good and evil, hot and cold, and other opposites are similarly related. In addition, he noted that a single substance may be perceived in opposing ways, thus, sea water is both harmful (for humans) and beneficial (for fishes).

The connection is the interaction between such opposing tendencies which enables us to unify tendencies which otherwise appear chaotic. Everything is unified in our account (or *logos*) of the changes around us. We see the balance and connectedness between things in our objective account of events. But nevertheless everything in the world is moving. Plato tells us: 'Heracleitus somewhere says that all things are in motion and nothing at rest; he compares them to the stream of a river, and says that you cannot step twice into the same river.'[7]

Seeing nothing but change and constant motion around him, Heracleitus concluded that fire must be the underlying substance of which everything is made or destroyed. Fire changes things by upward and downward paths. When fire is condensed it becomes moist, and under compression it turns into water. When water is congealed it is turned into earth. This is the downward path. When earth is liquefied, water emerges, and from that everything else is created by this process of evaporation from the sea. This is the upward path. Everything is in a dynamic state of change in which there is no stability or resting point.

Some of Heracleitus's other sayings are noteworthy:

- ➲ If you do not expect the unexpected, you will not find it; for it is hard to be sought and difficult.
- ➲ Eyes and ears are bad witnesses to men if they have souls that do not understand their language.
- ➲ Nature loves to hide.
- ➲ Man is called a baby by God, even as a child by man.
- ➲ The wisest man is an ape compared to God, just as the most beautiful ape is ugly compared to man.
- ➲ A man's character is his fate.
- ➲ Those who love wisdom must be good inquirers into many things.

Parmenides (c.515–c.440 bce)

Parmenides of Elea is another example of a highly practical philosopher who legislated for his city of Elea in the south of Italy. Long afterwards, the Eleans swore annually to abide by his laws.[8] He was allegedly the first to assert that the earth is spherical and situated in the centre of the universe.[9] Parmenides began as a Pythagorean but was outraged by Heracleitus and his violation of the law of contradiction. If there is no stability then the same things can be moving and not moving, or hot and cold at the same time. He objected strongly to this everchanging world and went to the other extreme by arguing that all change is an illusion. He concluded that the multiplicity of the existing things, their changing forms and motion, are only an appearance of a single eternal reality ('Being'), thus giving rise to the Parmenidean principle that 'all is one'. From this concept of Being, he deduced that all claims of change or of non-Being are illogical. In opposition to the Ionian natural philosophers who accepted the reality of change and looked for material stuff underlying it, Parmenides used an abstract, logical or generalised analysis to understand what we mean by 'to be'. To that extent, he may be regarded as the founder of metaphysics, and his use of the law of contradiction marked the introduction of logic as the prime method of philosophy. Plato's dialogue the *Parmenides* deals with his thought. He put his views forward in a long poem, a substantial proportion of which has been preserved. Here is a sample:

> Come now, I will tell you – preserve the account when you hear it –
> there are the only two roads of inquiry to be thought of:
> one, that it is and cannot not be,
> is the path of persuasion, (for truth accompanies it);
> another, that it is not and must not be –
> this I say to you is a path devoid of all knowledge
> For you could not recognise that which is not (for it is not to be done)
> nor could you mention it.[10]

Parmenides is arguing that when something exists then it is not possible for it not to exist. That which is, is, and it cannot more or less exist. If something does not exist then you can't know about it or say anything about it. This leads to the ambiguity of 'nothingness' which is still with us. We can say something meaningful such as 'there is nothing there', even though we don't know what the 'nothing' is or what it refers to. Thus, all the problems of negation and of modern logic in general stem from this single great advance in logical thinking.

Empedocles (c.490–c.430 BCE)

Empedocles of Acragas completed the natural philosophy developed by the Greeks by asserting that all matter was composed of four essential ingredients: fire, air, water and earth. This view of how the world is constituted survived till at least the seventeenth century. Hence the medieval system of 'humours' which we must balance to maintain our health:

Fire	hot and dry	choleric
Air	hot and moist	sanguine
Water	cold and moist	phlegmatic
Earth	cold and dry	melancholic

Zeno's paradoxes

Parmenides' pupil, Zeno of Elea (b. 490 BCE), produced his famous paradoxes to prove by logic that motion doesn't really exist. Consider an arrow in its flight. At any moment the arrow either is where it is or is where it is not. If it is where it is, it cannot be moving, since if it were moving, it would not be there, and it cannot be where it is not. Therefore, at that particular moment it is not moving. The same argument applies to every other point or moment in the arrow's flight. At no point or moment does it move, therefore its movement as a whole is an illusion. Similarly, when Achilles races against a tortoise and gives it a head start, he never really catches up with it. By the time that Achilles reaches point A, the tortoise has moved on to point B. Achilles would have to move through an infinity of points of time but that is logically impossible, therefore he doesn't really move at all, let alone catch up and pass the tortoise. These paradoxes offend our common sense but countering the logic behind them has occupied philosophers even down to the present day.

Empedocles was strongly influenced by Parmenides, who emphasised the unity of all things. He therefore argued that nothing either comes into being nor is destroyed but is merely transformed, depending on the ratio of basic substances, to one another. Like Heracleitus, he believed that two forces, Love and Strife, interact to bring together and to separate the four substances. Strife makes each of these elements withdraw itself from the others; Love makes them mingle together. The real world is at a stage in which neither force dominates. In the beginning, Love was dominant and all four substances were mixed together; during the formation of the cosmos, Strife entered to separate air, fire, earth and water from one another. Subsequently, the four elements were again arranged in partial combinations in certain places; springs and volcanoes, for example, show the presence of both water and fire in the earth. Empedocles believed in the transmigration of souls and declared that sinners must wander for 30,000 seasons through many mortal bodies and be tossed from one of the four elements to another. Escape from such punishment requires purification, particularly abstention from the flesh of animals, whose souls may once have inhabited human bodies.

Democritus (c.460–c.370 BCE)

Democritus of Abdera is famous for his 'atoms and the void' doctrines which anticipated approximately to modern atomic theory. It seems that he was a wealthy citizen of Abdera, in Thrace, that he travelled widely in the east, and that he lived to a great age. His physical and cosmological doctrines were an elaborated and systematised version of those of his teacher, Leucippus. To account for the changing physical world, Democritus asserted that space, or the Void, exists equally with the reality, or Being of physical objects. He regarded the Void as a vacuum, an infinite space in which moved an infinite number of atoms that made up Being (i.e. the physical world). Atoms were said to be:

⊃ eternal and invisible;

⊃ absolutely small, so that their size cannot be diminished (hence the name *atomon*, 'indivisible');

⊃ absolutely full and incompressible, being without pores and entirely filling the space they occupy;

⊃ homogeneous, differing only in shape, arrangement, position and magnitude.

While atoms differ in quantity, differences of quality are only apparent, owing to the impressions caused on our senses by different configurations and combinations of atoms. A thing is hot or cold, sweet or bitter, or hard or soft only by convention. The only things that exist in reality are atoms and the Void. Thus, the atoms of water and iron are the same, but those of water, being smooth and round and therefore unable to hook on to one another, roll over and over like small globes, whereas those of iron, being rough, jagged and uneven, cling together and form a solid body. Because all phenomena are composed of the same eternal atoms, nothing comes into being or perishes in the absolute sense of the words, although the compounds made out of the atoms are liable to increase and decrease, explaining a thing's appearance and disappearance, or 'birth' and 'death'.

Though Democritus' atomic theory was sheer speculation, it turned out to be remarkably correct. It was even accepted as a valid scientific theory by the nineteenth-century chemist John Dalton. However, the indivisibility of atoms was disproved by Rutherford's experimental splitting of the atom in 1908.

Democritus attributed popular belief in the gods to a desire to explain extraordinary phenomena (thunder, lightning, earthquakes) by reference to superhuman agency. His ethical system posited an ultimate good ('cheerfulness') that was 'a state in which the soul lives peacefully and tranquilly, undisturbed by fear or superstition or any other feeling'.[11]

The achievements of the early Greek philosophers

Thales	the first scientific hypothesis concerning the material basis of reality
Anaximander	the first evolutionary hypothesis concerning human origins
Anaximenes	the first systematic theory concerning the formation of matter
Pythagoras	the first systematic study of mathematics
Heracleitus	the first attempt to give an objective scientific account of everything
Parmenides	the first theory of valid logical deduction
Zeno	the first logical paradoxes
Empedocles	the first complete conservation theory of matter
Democritus	the first atomic theory of matter

The nature of early Greek speculation

The origins of philosophy among the early Greeks lay in their interactive social life in which conversation was uppermost. Philosophy arose as a highly speculative activity in which men talked about anything and everything. Plato has Parmenides giving the young Socrates the following advice:

> You must make an effort and submit yourself, while you are still young, to a severer training in what the world calls idle talk (ἀδολεσχίας) and condemns as useless. Otherwise, the truth will escape you.
>
> Plato, *Parmenides*[12]

According to Socrates, the great Athenian politician Pericles honed his political skills in the following manner:

> All great arts require idle talk and high-flown speculation (ἀδολεσχίας καὶ μετεωρολόγιας) about nature; for highmindedness and all-round abilities come from these pursuits. Now Pericles added these qualities to his own natural gifts; he fell in with Anaxagoras, who was a thinker of this type.
>
> Plato, *Phaedrus*[13]

Though there was great emphasis on 'idle talk' (*adoleschias*) and 'high-flown speculation' (*meteorologias*), there was equal emphasis on the practical application of speculation and on bringing it down-to-earth in some way or other. Amid all their philosophy, the Presocratic philosophers were, as we have seen, largely men of action who were politically active in their respective cities. There is a pay-off between philosophy and practicality when philosophy is pursued in an openminded and argumentative fashion.

Therefore, the distinctiveness of philosophy at its best may be summed up in the diagram illustrated below. Our inquiring and questioning often lead us into

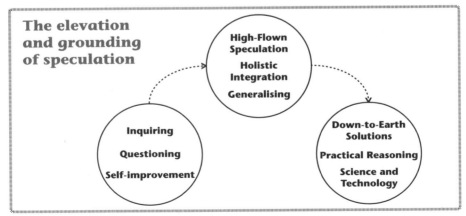

The elevation and grounding of speculation

High-Flown Speculation
Holistic Integration
Generalising

Inquiring
Questioning
Self-improvement

Down-to-Earth Solutions
Practical Reasoning
Science and Technology

stratospheric speculation but it must always come down to earth if it is to be of lasting use to us. Only interactive, dualistic thinking ensures that we can come down to earth. It combines high-flown idealistic speculation with the down-to-earth realism of practical application. Furthermore it moves from one to the other in a flexible and open-minded fashion which is not sustained either by extreme dogmatism or extreme scepticism, or by an exclusively empiricist or rationalist position.

Notes

1. Giorgio de Santillana (1961), *The Origins of Scientific Thought*, New York: New American Library, 1961, p. 21.
2. Translation as in G.S. Kirk and J.E. Raven (1957), *The Presocratic Philosophers*, Cambridge: Cambridge University Press, 1989, p. 107.
3. Carl Sagan (1981), *Cosmos*, London: Macdonald, 1984, pp. 236–7.
4. Cf. John Burnet (1930), *Early Greek Philosophy*, London: A. & C. Black, 1975, p. 100 n. 3.
5. Diogenes Laertius (*c.*300 CE), *Lives and Opinions of Eminent Philosophers*, Loeb Classical Library, London: Heinemann, 1980, Vol. I, Book II, Ch. 5, Socrates, §22, p. 153.
6. Translation as in G.S. Kirk and J.E. Raven (1957), *The Presocratic Philosophers*, p. 187.
7. Plato, *Cratylus*, 402a in *The Collected Dialogues of Plato*, ed. E. Hamilton and H. Cairns, Princeton: Princeton University Press, 1978, p. 439.
8. Cf. John Burnet (1930), Early Greek Philosophy, p. 171.
9. Diogenes Laertius, *Lives and Opinions of Eminent Philosophers*, Vol. II, Book IX, Ch. 3, Parmenides, §22, p. 431.
10. Greek text as in G.S. Kirk and J.E. Raven (1957), *The Presocratic Philosophers*, p. 269.
11. Diogenes Laertius, *Lives and Opinions of Eminent Philosophers*, Vol. II, Book IX, Ch. 7, Democritus, §45, p. 455.
12. Plato *Parmenides*, 135d, in *The Collected Dialogues of Plato*, p. 930.
13. Plato, *Phaedrus*, 269e 54, trans. W. Hamilton, Harmondsworth: Penguin, 1975, p. 89.

1.2 Classical Greek Philosophy

> Socrates took the initiative in summoning philosophy down from the heavens. He transferred it to the actual cities inhabited by mankind, and moved it right into people's own homes; and he compelled it to ask questions about how one ought to live and behave, and what is good and what is bad.
>
> Cicero[1]

Philosophy as we know it today really begins with the Classical Greek philosophers: Socrates, Plato and Aristotle. When we read about the thoughts and deeds of Socrates in Plato's dialogues we find a human being who would not be out of place in our complex modern society. Indeed, the culture and living standards of Athens in the fifth and fourth centuries BCE were not decisively overtaken in the western world till at least the end of the nineteenth century. To understand the aims and aspirations of western culture it is necessary to understand the philosophical advances achieved by these philosophers.

Socrates (c.470–399 BCE)

Socrates began as student of Ionian philosophy but he soon saw its limitations. His great insight came in seeing that moral philosophy was an area of thought that required as much development as natural philosophy. His philosophising consisted in examining our concepts, particularly moral concepts such as the good, virtue, justice, piety and courage. He therefore invented the study of ethics as a body of knowledge in its own right. He also believed in the benefits of self-knowledge. As Cicero says above, Socrates 'summoned philosophy down from the heavens'. That is to say, he moved philosophy *from* the nature speculation of the Ionian and Italian cosmologists *on to* the analyses of the character and conduct of human life, which he criticised by examining such notions as the good, virtue and justice. Living during the chaos of the Peloponnesian War, with its erosion of moral values, Socrates advocated the ethical life by his admonition to 'know thyself'. Only by reviewing our own conduct, making ourselves aware of its nature and consequences for others, and changing our behaviour accordingly, can we be said to be living morally.

In his youth (as Plato's dialogues show), Socrates closely studied the works of philosophers. In later life, he dedicated himself, body and soul, to debating philosophy with his fellow Athenians. He was famous for the intensity with which he philosophised. He is reputed to have spent a whole day and night standing in the open air, deep in thought over some philosophical problem.[2]

He was an immensely talented thinker who deliberately avoided writing his thoughts down. He believed that his role as a philosopher was to walk around talking and arguing with people in the public places of Athens. He spent his spare time wrapped in thought by which he unified his thinking. This ensured that he was always 'on the ball' in his conversations and discussions. He is the ultimate example of a street philosopher who philosophised among the people and not in academic isolation.

Socrates was fortunate enough to be born in Athens at the time of its cultural explosion during the fifth century BCE. In his youth, he met the great Parmenides when the latter visited Athens with Zeno of Elea. He also argued with sophists such as Protagoras when they visited Athens to lecture rich young men on citizenship. These encounters are recorded in Plato's dialogues, *Parmenides* and *Protagoras*.

The trial of Socrates

Socrates' immortality was assured by the way he died at the hands of Athenian democracy. He was made a scapegoat for the unpopularity of the sophists who taught young men and allegedly put them against their families. He was also regarded with suspicion because of his privileged access to a divine spirit telling him what to think; what we might now call his intuitions from the unconscious mind. He was therefore charged with 'corrupting the minds of young people' and with 'believing in gods not recognised by the city'. If he had pleaded guilty he might have been exiled into private life. But he defended himself obstinately and claimed that it was his divine mission to practise philosophy and question everyone's beliefs and opinions since he himself knew nothing. When he was found guilty, he suggested that instead of being punished for his behaviour he should be rewarded as a public benefactor and maintained by the city for the rest of his life. Failing that, he should be fined a paltry sum of money. His apparent arrogance outraged the jury of citizens and they voted to condemn him to death by poison. Socrates readily obeyed the verdict of the court and refused to allow his friends to arrange his release or to escape into exile. His death was regretted by the city and an outpouring of writings by his disciples including Plato and Xenophon defended his reputation. His example was important to western culture for two diametrically opposing reasons. It shows (1) the need to stand up for ourselves against hostile public opinion, and (2) the need to conform to the norms and laws of society. Balancing these irreconcilable positions has often provided the dynamic for progress in our culture. There are obvious parallels between the martyrdom of Socrates and fate of Jesus Christ at the hands of the authorities. This helped the early Christians to establish the dominance of Christianity throughout the Roman Empire.

He was not particularly fashionable in his own lifetime. Apart from the young men who were his disciples, most people in Athens regarded him as a nuisance as he was always questioning them. This led to his famous trial which he refused to take seriously. He became extremely fashionable immediately after his state execution and he continued to be so during classical times. Through the work of his disciples, his importance came to be appreciated by the Athenians. His influence on the wealthy young men of Athens was exhaustively chronicled in the dialogues of Plato and Xenophon, which were written to absolve Socrates from the false accusations made against him.

Socrates' greatness as a philosopher lay in his acknowledging the extent of his ignorance and in his influence on his disciples. He avoided writing probably because he did not wish to commit himself to particular views. What we understand about them is to be found chiefly in the early dialogues of Plato. He therefore did not work out his philosophy to make it presentable to the public at large, and he gave his pupils no fixed views to follow. In fact, the inconclusive nature of his views perhaps makes him the first of the sceptical Greek philosophers. Ironically, his disciples tended to go to the other extreme and they became dogmatic philosophers.

Plato (c.427–c.347 BCE)

Plato's real name was 'Aristocles'. He was given the nickname 'Platonos', apparently referring to his squat or 'flat' appearance.[3] In contrast with Socrates, Plato's talents lay more in writing rather than in speaking. He composed subtle and inventive dialogues in which he expounded his philosophical views. He is famed for the unsurpassed literary style in which he put forward his ideas. He made Socrates his mouthpiece in most of his dialogues. In his early short dialogues, he may be expressing the kind of views put forward by Socrates, but clearly in dialogues such as *The Republic* he is putting his own elaborate views which go far beyond the sceptical views of Socrates. Plato not only benefited from the intellectual hothouse of Athens during its zenith, he was also a committed disciple of Socrates whose views he imbibed and developed further in his own writings.

Plato instituted the first 'Academy', which was a model for philosophical schools throughout the classical period. He was therefore literally the first 'academic philosopher' as his philosophy was not for the public in general. He wrote not only lengthy dialogues but also gave lectures in his Academy. None of these lectures has been preserved and we only have skimpy details concerning their content. Plato's greatest achievement was in reconciling the philosophies of Heracleitus and Parmenides. The former saw the world as consisting of nothing but change and movement. Parmenides reacted against this extreme view by stressing the unity of things in which movement is not possible. Plato reconciled these extremes by assigning change and movement to perceptual appearances, and stability and eternity to the forms or ideas of things. His theory of forms or ideas implies that our ideas of tables and chairs exist as perfect objects in their own right. What we perceive are not real things but only copies of these ideas which exist in eternity and are therefore out of our reach altogether. By giving our ideas such a divine status, he makes them more important than human beings. Even today, people with extreme political and religious views confer a Platonic reality on their ideas that makes them worth fighting and killing people for. It is surely better to regard our ideas as flexible tools that reflect our human limitations rather than a divine realm beyond our reach.

Plato was fashionable throughout the period of antiquity but he fell out of favour with Christians because his views were seen as sceptical in an age that craved belief and faith. A revival of interest in his dialogues began in Renaissance times when the ideal of Platonic love became fashionable.

His influence on subsequent thinkers has been immense and it endures up to the present day. 'The European philosophical tradition consists of a series of footnotes to Plato',[4] so said A.N. Whitehead who was himself a Platonist. This is not entirely true in that the empiricist movement has progressively moved away from an adherence to fixed Platonic ideas existing who knows where.

Plato's philosophy was limited in that he explained everything in terms of his theory of forms. But even he recognised the limitations to that theory in his dialogue *Parmenides*. His legacy has also been negative in that his dialogue, *The Republic*, lays down the model for a class-ridden, authoritarian type of society that has recurred throughout the history of western culture.

Plato's The Republic

This is generally considered to be Plato's finest work, even though his views are no longer as persuasive as they once were. Its name is the Latin rendering (*res publica* – public matters) of the Greek *politeia* meaning 'constitution' or 'government'. Understanding the flaws in Plato's *The Republic* is important today, because all the authoritarian regimes of the twentieth century followed Plato's reasonings and assumptions about human nature and how people must be governed.

The first book of *The Republic* seems to be an early work in which Socrates deals inconclusively with the notion of justice. At the end of that book, Socrates confesses his usual ignorance of the subject because he can't be sure what makes a person just, virtuous or good. But he does argue strongly against the 'right is might' view, which is relevant today when fanatics attempt to enforce their views on us with weapons and bombs. The unjust person may disregard the law and use force to get his way. But this means that everyone fights each other instead of co-operating to make their own contribution to society. A just society works by enabling people to co-operate instead of competing with each other.

A just person for the Greeks was not just a fair or law-abiding person. He held also to the right way of living and fitted into the life of his city. Plato takes up this theme in the later books of *The Republic* and describes in detail what a just society should be like. It is a society in which everyone has their place and knows what their role in life is to be. In other words, *The Republic* describes the original utopian or ideal society to which we must aspire if we are to have a truly rational and workable society. Such utopianism is now regarded with deep suspicion following the attempts of twentieth-century dictators to impose ideal societies by authoritarian means.

In *The Republic* a rigid class system is laid down in which people are born to be 'golden' rulers, 'silver' soldiers or 'iron' or 'bronze' farmers and workers. Unrealistically, the rulers are to have no property of their own and to live austere Spartan lives. They have their wives and children in common and 'golden' women are educated to be rulers alongside men. The rulers must be content with their intellectual superiority by which they alone have access to the Truth and the Good Life. The rest are to be given 'noble lies' to keep them mute and contented.[5]

The Republic is notable for two myths: the myth of the cave and the myth of Er.

The myth of the cave[6]
According to Plato, most people live in darkness knowing very little about what is really happening in the world. It is as if they were prisoners chained together in a cave since childhood and unable to see behind them. They hear sounds and see the shadows of figures reflected by a fire behind them. These are all the reality which is available to them. If a prisoner is released and taken outside into the dazzling sun, he would have difficulty comprehending what he is now seeing. Nothing would be true to his previous experience of things. He would need time to accustom himself and understand what the sun is. If he were to take this knowledge back to his fellow prisoners they would not believe or understand him. They would think that he had taken leave of his senses by going out of the cave since, to them, the upper world had nothing to teach them.

Plato argues that the philosopher rulers are like the released man when they learn the superior knowledge to be gained by understanding the ideas or forms of things. He says that 'the highest form of knowledge is knowledge of the good from which all things that are just derive their usefulness and value'.[7] Whereas ordinary people are concerned with the visible world governed by the sun, the philosopher enters the intelligible world governed by the good which is the source of our useful knowledge. Thus, the philosopher is fit to rule people because he alone knows what is good for them. Such confidence in philosophers is scarcely credible nowadays.

The myth of Er[8]
The last book of *The Republic* concerns the immortality of the soul and its treatment after death. It is important because later Christian doctrine adopted wholesale this view of heaven, hell and the afterlife. Er was allegedly killed in

battle but came back to life on his funeral pyre (what we might call 'a near-death experience'). He said that he had been assigned by the immortal judges to inform men about the afterlife. His story was that when the soul leaves the body of a 'just' man it is judged accordingly and goes up to heaven to be cleansed and purified. The unjust soul travels underground and is punished tenfold for its misdeeds. Thereafter, the souls are reborn into mortal life after drawing lots and making choices according to the selections laid before them. Their choices depend on how well or badly they lived their lives previously. The better we live our lives now, the more this will hold us in good stead in our future lives. Before being reborn, the souls drink of the river of forgetfulness (*Lethe*) so that after rebirth they remember nothing of their past lives. Er was told not to drink from the river. All this shows the strength of Plato's poetical imagination. No doubt his Myth of Atlantis was similarly a work of imagination.[9]

//

Plato's Dialogues

Plato's early dialogues	The last days of Socrates	Plato's later dialogues
Charmides – temperance	*Euthyphro* – piety	*Critias* – the myth of Atlantis
Cratylus – language	*Apology* – court defence	*Gorgias* – the good life
Euthydemus – education	*Crito* – state conformity	*Laws* – the ultimate legal system
Ion – art and poetry	*Phaedo* – immortality	*Meno* – the teachability of virtue
Laches – courage		*Parmenides* – the theory of ideas
Lysis – friendship		*Philebus* – pleasure and wisdom
Phaedrus – truth and beauty		*The Republic* (Bks 2–10) – the ideal society
Protagoras – virtue		*Sophist* – the role of the philosopher
The Republic (Bk 1) – justice		*Statesman* – logical definitions
Symposium – love		*Theaetetus* – knowledge and belief
		Timaeus – man and the universe

Aristotle (384–322 BCE)

Aristotle was the ultimate polymath who was interested in everything and wrote about it (unlike Socrates who was interested in everything but wrote nothing). His particular interest was biology which made him keen on classifying and categorising things. As a result, he laid down the foundations for distinct bodies of knowledge that are still with us today. These include logic, ethics, politics, metaphysics, psychology, physics, theology and meteorology. His output was truly prodigious. Apart from the writings that have come down to us, Aristotle also wrote a number of dialogues which have been lost apart from quotations and references to them.

When Aristotle came to Athens, he became a disciple of Plato and this gave him the background that he required to grow intellectually. He arrived at innumerable insights, many of which changed western thinking for ever. For instance, he clarified the distinction between potential and actual which is still indispensable to us today. Although he began as Plato's disciple, he criticised the theory of forms and preferred to think in terms of universals attached to words rather than ideas existing eternally. Thus, the word 'table' applies universally to objects that are essentially tables, and there is no idea of a table existing independently of tables in general. This view became known as 'nominalism' as opposed to Plato's 'realism'.

Aristotle was famous for being the tutor of Alexander the Great, whom he may have helped to think big, and be confident and driven enough to conquer the east as far as India. Through his influence on Alexander, Aristotle effectively ensured the dominance of Greek culture (during the Hellenist period) until the Romans took over.

Aristotle was perhaps less fashionable than Plato during the Hellenist and Roman periods. But his writings were especially appreciated by Muslim scholars who bequeathed their interest to the scholastic philosophers of the medieval period. These scholars were particularly interested in Aristotle's theological views. They preserved most of Aristotle's works throughout the Dark Ages and ensured the revival of interest in his philosophy from the 900s onwards. Western thinking has been very largely Aristotelian in its logical thinking right down to the present day.

The deficiencies in Aristotle's philosophy were made clear from the seventeenth century onwards. The scientific revolution showed his *Physics* to be erroneous because he reasoned out the nature of things instead of experimenting and using trial-and-error procedures to find out how things really work. His logic remained uncriticised until the end of the nineteenth century when symbolic logic was developed and the scope of logic greatly expanded over that bequeathed from Aristotle. To some extent, western thinking has been stultified by the limited nature of his logic, and this deficiency has recently been exploited by postmodern philosophers such as Derrida.

Aristotle's Organon

The *Organon* was the name given to Aristotle's books on logic. It means 'tool' in Greek and later scholars saw his logic as being a 'tool' for doing philosophy. The six books forming the *Organon* are: *The Categories, On Interpretation, Prior Analytics, Posterior Analytics, Topics* and the *Sophistical Refutations*. Apart from the *Organon*, the fourth book of the *Metaphysics* also forms part of his logical work as it is mainly concerned with the general principles of thought, namely, the principles of identity and non-contradiction, and the law of the excluded middle. Aristotle's own name for logic was 'analytics'. He invented the science of logic from scratch as he said in almost the only personal statement to be found in his writings: 'Regarding reasoning [or syllogising], we had absolutely no earlier work to quote but were for a long time labouring at tentative researches.'[10]

➲ In **The Categories**, Aristotle argues that subjects of sentences predicate things in one or another of the following categories: substance, quantity, quality, relation, place, time, position, state, action and affection. These categories give us the 'essence' of any object. The essence gives us the definitions on which formal logic is based.

➲ **On Interpretation** contains a pioneering account of 'modal' sentences ('It is possible that . . .'; 'It is necessary that . . .') and a celebrated discussion of future events such as the sea battle paradox.[11] If it is already true that there will be a sea battle tomorrow, then how can the battle be considered a contingent event? For if the truth is already determined, surely the battle is fixed and necessary? Aristotle's answer to this is that certain types of sentences about the future are neither true nor false.

➲ The **Prior Analytics** lays the foundations of his syllogistic logic as it deals with the various forms of 'syllogism' such as 'All men are mortal, Socrates is a man, therefore Socrates is mortal.' The syllogism grounds logic on how words are defined and applied to objects. 'Man' is defined as a mortal being and is referred to as being a 'man'. Logic therefore expects too much as it demands total agreement about the definitions and use of words and sentences.

➲ The **Posterior Analytics** is devoted to demonstrative arguments and the theory of 'definition', Aristotle thought that the most important axioms of any science are the definitions of its subject matter. For example, among the axioms of geometry there is a definition of the triangle, which is an account of what a triangle really is or of the essence of a triangle. Thus, Aristotle saw all the sciences as being based on demonstrative or deductive reasoning like geometry. He paid less attention to inductive reasoning or how we arrive at general or overall views of things.

➲ In the **Sophistical Refutations**, Aristotle exposes forms of reasoning that appear valid on the surface but are in fact fallacious or plain wrong. Examples of fallacious arguments are: (1) *petitio principii* – 'begging the question' or circular argument (e.g. a 'proof' that the soul continues to exist after death because it is immortal); (2) *argumentum ad hominem* which attacks the person and not that person's argument or beliefs; (3) the 'fallacy of the consequent' or arguing from a consequent to its condition (e.g. if a man is a drunkard, he becomes destitute; Peter is destitute: therefore Peter is a drunkard); and (4) the 'fallacy of the irrelevant conclusion' in which, instead of proving the fact in dispute, the arguer seeks to gain their point by diverting attention to some extraneous fact.

⊃ The ***Topics*** is perhaps best placed last as it deals with the general rules of argumentation. It includes many miscellaneous matters needed to complete Aristotle's comprehensive account of logic.

Aristotle's Metaphysics

The word 'metaphysics' comes from the Greek *meta ta physica* meaning 'after the physics', as the book was placed after the book called 'the physics' in the early listings of his books. His own name for the book was 'first philosophy'. He begins by stating that: 'All human beings by nature desire to know.' Wisdom consists in knowing what lies behind things and 'the science which knows to what end each thing must be done is the most authoritative of the sciences' and 'this must be a science that investigates the first principles and causes'.[12]

As regards first principles, first, the nature of Plato's forms is investigated and Aristotle details twenty-three objections and criticisms of the theory of forms.[13] Secondly, we need to understand 'being as being' that is, the beingness of things, or what is it for something to exist or not exist.[14] This has been the subject of ontology in modern times. This means examining the different senses of the verb 'to be', the existence of numbers, the nature of oddness and evenness, the nature of substance and so on.[15]

Aristotle was the first philosopher to clarify the four causes of things: the material, formal, efficient and final causes.[16] Thus, a statue is made of bronze and this is its *material* cause. It is shaped into a certain form by the sculptor and this is its *formal* cause. The thought, skill and tools that the sculptor needs to make the statue are its *efficient* cause. The sculptor's aims and intentions in making the statue are its *final* cause. These distinctions involve a broader use of the word 'cause' than scientific causes which are concerned with material and efficient causes, that is to say, what things are made of and what we can or cannot do with them, as well as the connection between a cause and its effect.

Aristotle was also the first philosopher to make the important metaphysical distinction between potentiality and actuality.[17] Things exist potentially until they are actually made or become what they can become. An acorn has the potential to become a mighty oak tree. It has the power, potency and possibility to become so. But whether it actually becomes an oak tree depends on such conditions as its fertility, its being put in the correct growing conditions, and so on. Clarifying this distinction contributed to the development of western culture as it ensures that we work out clearly what can or cannot be done, and what can really be achieved. In other words, practical and businesslike thinking depends of our making these distinctions.

In Aristotle's view, the existence and nature of God is also a metaphysical question. Whereas Plato saw God as the 'artificer' or architect of the universe,[18]

Aristotle regarded God as the prime mover or unmoved mover who gets things going, and is the first and final cause of everything.[19] Aristotle's God is not a personal God interested in the affairs of this world. He is pure intelligence, completely indifferent to the vicissitudes of the world, whose 'thinking is a thinking of thinking'.[20] Also, the prime mover is not to be understood in a temporal sense. He is not the creator of the world, as Aristotle thought that the world was not created at all but had existed for all eternity. The prime mover is the fountain-head of all motion. In that sense, he is the ultimate cause of everything that happens in the world.

Aristotle's Ethics

Aristotle's *Nicomachean Ethics* was written as a preliminary work to his book on *Politics*. He is mainly concerned with the behaviour of the human being as a *zoon politikon*, a city-dwelling animal (not a 'political animal' in our sense).[21] He begins his book by defining the good as 'that at which all things aim'. Studying what is the supreme good for man is the aim of the science of politics as we can only live a good life in a community such as a city. We all ought to aspire to the good life as our happiness depends on it. He distinguishes three ways of living the good life and achieving happiness: (1) a life of pleasure or enjoyment; (2) a life of social activity; and (3) a life of contemplative activity.[22] The last two may be distinguished as an active and a passive way of life as follows:

an active good life	**a passive good life**
involves:	*involves:*
social conformity	common sense
fitting into society	balanced living
learning skills and wisdom	the golden mean
becoming a great-souled person	becoming a contented person
taking an active role in society	indulging in a contemplative life
aiming for:	*aiming for:*
virtue or excellence	**happiness or well-being**

These ways of life are not clearly distinguished in the *Ethics* and we may well have both ways in our daily lives, just as we blend work and play, not to mention the scientific and religious attitudes. Moreover, the active life can lead to happiness or well-being just as the passive good life can lead to virtue or excellence. Each way of life only aims in one direction or the other.

Happiness is the usual translation for Aristotle's word *eudaimonia*, which really means 'good spiritedness' or 'well-being'. Happiness does not mean a temporary state of euphoria such as that induced by drink, drugs or other forms of mindless excitement. It is a balanced state of mind which we reach as a result of living a good life. 'Happiness is found to be something perfect and self-sufficient, being the end to which our actions are directed.'[23] In other words, we find happiness, for instance, in having done a good job.

Virtue is the translation of the Greek *aretê* which also means 'excellence' or 'efficiency'. Virtue is partly learnt by instruction and experience. It also means adopting and maintaining the correct habits of behaviour and becoming morally good.[24] We are not virtuous at birth but we are endowed with the capacity or disposition for becoming virtuous in the course of time. For example, a child begins by following his or her parents' instructions to tell the truth without being aware of the moral excellence of this action. Eventually, the habit of truth-telling becomes an ingrained part of the child's moral character.

Aristotle argues that virtue can be destroyed by having too much or too little of anything. He famously advocates a middle way or 'golden mean' between these. Virtue lies between the vicious extremes of excess and deficiency. For example, the virtue of courage is the mean between the excess of rashness and the deficiency of cowardice. Temperance lies between the excess of licentiousness and the deficiency of insensibility (or lack of feeling).[25] The problem with such neat calculations is that it is often unclear in practice where the middle way lies. What seemed courageous at the time may turn out to be rash or cowardly. Furthermore, we may need to go to extremes in our behaviour to find our way forward. The 'golden mean' is an interesting intellectual exercise but it is not enough to live by.

//

The development of schools of philosophy

Schools of philosophy in ancient Greece developed from the popular lectures of sophists or wise men who made a name for themselves throughout Greece by visiting the various cities and giving lectures to crowds of young men. Their role was to prepare them to be effective citizens in their communities. The sophists expected to be paid for their services and this gave rise to education as a profession in its own right. Both Plato and Aristotle criticised the sophists for teaching young men to be clever and manipulative speakers instead of wise and good citizens.

Subsequently, intellectual life in classical Greece and Rome became dominated by the various schools of philosophy which developed from the time of Plato and Aristotle onwards. Plato founded his school in the Academy in Athens and Aristotle in the Lyceum. Plato's successors were known as 'academics' and Aristotle's as 'peripatetics' because of Aristotle's habit of lecturing while walking round the gardens of the Lyceum. The Stoic School became very prominent and it paved the way for Christianity. The Stoics originally taught at the 'Portico' (the *Stoa Poikile* or Painted Colonnade) near the Athenian *agora* (marketplace), and the Epicureans in the Garden (*Ho Kipos*) in Athens. These schools generally were the focus of dogmatic philosophy where disciples were taught the works of the respective masters and there was little scope for deviation from their doctrines.

The Stoics

The Stoic movement was founded at Athens around 300 BCE by Zeno (334–262 BCE) of Citium in Cyprus (not to be confused with the earlier Zeno of Elea). Stoicism was influential throughout the Greek and Roman periods up to at least 200 CE. The Stoics argued that the good for man is not health, wealth or anything that identifies happiness with worldly success. Virtue is beneficial and consists in a wholesome state of mind whereas vice is harmful and involves an unwholesome state of mind. Everything that doesn't involve the pursuit of virtue and the avoidance of vice is indifferent or unnecessary to our happiness. Thus, wealth or health, for example, can be used well or badly. Virtue gives us all that we need for happiness. If we are morally weak, we can never be completely unhappy, no matter how well off we are. Happiness and unhappiness don't depend on our genes, upbringing, or other chance occurrences of life. Our reasoning powers give us all we need to live well. Giving way to our emotions is an unhealthy state of mind. The virtuous person doesn't give way to fear, desire, grief, despair or other emotions because they are always in complete possession of their faculties. In being virtuous we are impregnable to the vicissitudes of fortune. The Stoic School paved the way for Christianity which adopted and applied the forbearance, obedience to authority, and cheek-turning which were characteristic of Stoicism. Prominent Roman Stoics included Seneca (*c.*5 BCE–65 CE), Epictetus (born *c.*50 CE), and Marcus Aurelius (212–275 CE). Cicero (106–43 BCE) was not himself a Stoic but he discussed stoical doctrines in his writings.

Epicurus (341–270 BCE)

Epicurus was born on Samos but educated in Athens. He became a student of the Democritean atomic theory and later adopted it into his philosophy. He allegedly wrote over 300 works but most of these have been lost. Epicurus believed that the proper goal of life was pleasure. But he was not a mere hedonist or pleasure seeker, as he defined pleasure austerely as the absence of discomfort or pain. He ate to rid himself of the discomfort of hunger and no more. The essence of his philosophy was to run away from life because it involves too much pain. We can only avoid grief at the death of a close friend by having no close friends. We can never be satisfied with our desire for wealth, power, and fame, therefore we should avoid them. The wise man should avoid politics as it may threaten the tranquillity of his soul. In spite of the egoistic nature of his philosophy, Epicurus emphasised the importance of friendship but only in that a wise man loves his friend as much as he loves himself. His philosophy was systematically worked out in terms of the scientific knowledge of his day. Its breadth and scale can be seen in Lucretius' *The Nature of Things* in which Epicurean philosophy is expounded in Latin verse. An Epicurean school of philosophy was established by the Greek scholar Philodemus around 80 BCE in what is now known as 'The

Villa of the Papyri' at Herculaneum. Many charred papyrus scrolls of Epicurean writings have been found in this villa, having been preserved by the 79 CE eruption of Mount Vesuvius. More works of Epicurus may yet be found in the lower, unexcavated floors of the villa, as well as lost classics.[26]

The schools of philosophy in later antiquity

Significantly, there were no more great philosophers in classical antiquity after the Romans imposed their governor on Macedonia in 146 BCE. The Romans later extended their hold over the whole of Greece and reduced the great cities of Greece to ruins, as later Roman visitors recorded. However, the Greeks responded in a civilised way by making a cultural conquest of Rome, as its scholars were increasingly used to teach the Romans the language and philosophy of Greece. By the time of Cicero Roman aristocrats spoke Greek among themselves. The strength of Greek culture is shown by the fact that the Eastern Roman Empire remained Greek-speaking till it ended after the fall of Constantinople in 1453 CE.

The elitist culture of the Roman Empire meant that the schools of philosophy became associated with places like Athens, Rhodes and Alexandria, or they were patronised by wealthy Roman aristocrats. For example, it is thought that the Epicurean school of Philodemus mentioned above was patronised by L. Calpurnius Piso, Consul of Rome in 58 BCE and father-in-law of Julius Caesar.

Instead of progressing in an open-minded fashion which was later characteristic of science, most philosophers tended to become either sceptics or dogmatists. Indeed, Diogenes Laertius (*c.*300 CE, and the author of the only complete 'Lives of the Philosophers' to come down to us) states: 'Philosophers may be divided into dogmatists and sceptics: dogmatists are all those who make assertions about things assuming that they can be known; while sceptics are those who suspend their judgment on the ground that things are unknowable.'[27] It is arguable that this very dichotomy prevented the development of scientific method till the seventeenth century with the works of Bacon and the experiments of Galileo.

In antiquity, scholars had only three alternatives in their intellectual development: They could either (1) belong to or establish a dogmatic school of philosophy such as the Peripatetics, Stoics or Epicureans; or (2) become sceptics like the Pyrrhonians or the Middle and New Academic scholars; or (3) become eclectic scholars like Cicero (106-43 BCE) and Plutarch (*c.*46-*c.*120 CE) who studied all philosophies without adhering to any particular one. Eclectics were chroniclers of philosophy who made no attempt to reconcile or combine these doctrines. Such a reconciliation would have been a *syncretism*, which Plato achieved in reconciling the opposing philosophies of Heracleitus and Parmenides. Some Academic, Stoic and Epicurean philosophers also adopted an eclectic approach in their teachings. Cicero's Latin writings were responsible for broadening Latin vocabulary to cope with the technical terms of Greek philosophers.

The stagnant and élitist nature of philosophy meant that most people in the Roman Empire knew little and cared less about philosophy. Their philosophical naivety made them virgin territory on which the seeds of religion took root and flourished until Christianity proved to be the most dominant and resilient religion of all. The intellectual conditions in antiquity increasingly favoured dogmatism over any sceptical doubts. As a result, when Christianity came to the fore, it meant the complete triumph of dogmatism over both scepticism and eclecticism, and the eventual demise of philosophy in general. Noteworthy philosophical movements such as Neoplatonism and Gnosticism thrived only in so far as they contributed to the religiosity and god belief of the times.

Christianity triumphed over philosophy because people craved for certainty and despised the uncertainties and equivocations offered by intellectuals. The Roman Empire was falling apart and the certainties of religion were the only bulwark against the uncertainties of the times they lived in. People wanted to be told what to think rather than think for themselves. When the barbarians marched into Italy they found the cities depopulated and the countryside teeming with monasteries and nunneries. Gibbon reports that whole legions of Roman soldiers retreated into monasteries, presumably on the pretext of their religiosity.[28] This extremism did not happen in the Eastern Roman Empire because the strength of Greek culture meant that Christianity was assimilated in a much more moderate way. Thus, the Eastern Empire survived almost another thousand years.

The last noted scholar in the Western Empire was Ancius Boethius (c.480–524 CE). He became a Consul in 510 CE and served as adviser to Theodoric, the King of the Ostrogoths in Italy. He was imprisoned by Theodoric for his alleged sympathies towards the Eastern Roman Emperor's right to rule over the West. While in prison he wrote his classic work, *The Consolations of Philosophy*, which is still widely read today. It is largely a Platonic work extolling the virtues of Platonic ideals and putting faith in Providence and the afterlife.[29]

The schools of Athens were closed by the Emperor Justinian in 529 CE, and many scholars departed with their personal libraries for the court of the Persian king, Khosrow I, who was a great patron of culture. Thus, their books and works were subsequently used and diffused by Mohammedan scholars from the seventh century CE onwards.

The Alexandrian schools may have lasted till 563 CE before they were closed and the last scholars there, who had Christian names such as John and Elias, tried desperately to save the works of Plato and Aristotle by showing in their commentaries that these philosophers were believers and not the deadly sceptics that they were popularly believed to be. But it was to no avail, and religious fanaticism ensured that Dark Age ignorance and superstition prevailed in the end.

//

Learned women in antiquity

We hear little about the role of women in philosophy and intellectual affairs. Those we know about were not treated very respectfully.

Aspasia of Miletus (c.400 BCE) was the mistress of the Athenian statesman Pericles and a vivid figure in Athenian society. Her private life was publicly attacked, especially in the comedies of the period, and she was rumoured to have influenced Pericles in his political decisions. Like Socrates, she charged with impiety but was acquitted. Because she was foreign by birth, her son by Pericles, also called 'Pericles', was excluded by law from public affairs until he was made a citizen by a special act. He later became a general.

According to Xenophon in his *Memoirs of Socrates*, Aspasia was a personal friend of Socrates and he approved of her saying that 'good matchmakers were expert at bringing people together in matrimony by giving them true reports of their good qualities, and they refused to sing their praises falsely, because the victims of such deceptions hated both each other and the woman who arranged the match'.[30] Also, in the dialogue *Menexenus*, which is doubtfully attributed to Plato, Socrates says that he believes Aspasia composed Pericles's famous funeral oration in which he praises Athenian Democracy. This oration is recorded (or reconstructed) by Thucydides in his *History of the Peloponnesian War*.[31] The assertion that Aspasia composed this oration is not taken seriously by scholars, as Pericles was well capable of writing his own speeches.[32]

Axiothea and Lasthenia: Axiothea was said to have read Plato's *Republic*, adopted male dress and gone to study under Plato. Her name and that of another female pupil, Lasthenia, are only known to us because they exemplified the practice of Plato's theory of sexual equality in education as stated in *The Republic*.

Aretê of Cyrene (c.375 BCE) was the daughter of Aristippus of Cyrene, a follower of Socrates. Aretê is thought to have been the successor of her father as head of the Cyrenaic school, which taught that bodily pleasure is the chief good. Her son was nicknamed 'Mother-taught', indicating that she was his principal teacher.

Hipparchia the Cynic (c.300 BCE) is the only woman given a 'life' of her own in the early *Lives of the Philosophers* by Diogenes Laertius.[33] But we are told only gossip about her and nothing about her philosophy except that she adopted the cynical philosophy of her husband Crates. She defied convention to marry her husband, was completely devoted to him, and dressed in similar clothes.

Hypatia of Alexandria (c.370–415 CE) was a Neoplatonist philosopher who lived in Egypt and was the first known woman to achieve eminence in mathematics. She became the recognised head of the Neoplatonist school of philosophy at Alexandria, and attracted many pupils with her eloquence, modesty and beauty, as well as her remarkable intellectual gifts. Her published works have been lost but they included mathematical commentaries and a commentary on Ptolemy's astronomy. Letters written by a scholar, Synesius, record that he consulted her about the construction of an astrolabe and a hydroscope. Her philosophical writings were more scholarly and scientific than the mystical and sceptical writings of the Athenian Schools at that time.

During her lifetime, philosophy and learning in general were associated by the early Christians with paganism. She therefore became the focal point of tension and riots between Christians and non-Christians that racked Alexandria. After Cyril became patriarch of Alexandria in 412, the tensions increased and Hypatia was barbarously murdered by Nitrian monks and a fanatical mob of Cyril's Christian followers. The motive was supposedly her intimacy with Orestes, the city's pagan prefect. This event precipitated the departure of many scholars and marked the beginning of the decline of Alexandria as a major centre of ancient learning. She is the last of the known women philosophers until at least the Middle Ages.

Notes

1. Cicero (*c*.44 BCE), *On The Good Life*, trans. Michael Grant, Harmondsworth: Penguin, 1971, p. 57.
2. Plato, *Symposium*, trans. W. Hamilton, Harmondsworth: Penguin, 1978, 219e, pp. 108–9.
3. Cf. Diogenes Laertius, *Lives and Opinions of Eminent Philosophers*, Loeb Classical Library, London: Heinemann, 1980, Vol. I, Book III, Plato, §4, p. 279.
4. Alfred North Whitehead (1929), *Process and Reality*, New York: Free Press, 1978, Part II, ch. I, p. 39.
5. Plato, *The Republic*, trans. D. Lee, Harmondsworth: Penguin, 1974, Book III, 414c, p. 181. (Ψευδομένους πεῖσαι is usually translated as 'noble lie' and not 'magnificent myth' as here.)
6. Ibid., Book VI, 514a–517b, pp. 317–20.
7. Ibid., Book VI, 505a, p. 303.
8. Ibid., Book X, 608e–621d, pp. 440–55.
9. The Myth of Atlantis is mentioned, first of all, at the beginning of the dialogue, *Timaeus*, and then is detailed in the dialogue, *Critias*.
10. Aristotle, *Sophistical Refutations*, Sect. XXXIV, 184b, Loeb Classical Library, London: Heinemann, 1992, Vol. III, p. 155.
11. Aristotle, *On Interpretation*, Sect. IX, 18b24, Loeb Classical Library, London: Heinemann, 1949, Vol. I, p. 135.
12. Aristotle, *Metaphysics*, Book I, ch. 2, 982b, in *The Basic Works of Aristotle*, ed. R. McKeon, New York: Random House, 1941, p. 692.
13. Ibid., Book I, ch. 9, 990b, p. 706.
14. Ibid., Book IV, ch. 1, 1003a, p. 731, and Book VI, ch. 1, 1028a, pp. 783–4.
15. Ibid., Book IV, ch. 1, 1003b–4b, pp. 732–3.
16. Ibid., Book V, ch. 1, 1013a, p. 752.
17. Ibid., Book IX, ch. 1, 1046a, pp. 820–1.
18. Plato, *Timaeus*, trans. D. Lee, Harmondsworth: Penguin, 1969, 28, p. 40.
19. Aristotle, *Metaphysics*, Book XII, chs. 8–9, 1073a–1075a, in *The Basic Works of Aristotle*, ed. R. McKeon, New York: Random House, 1941, pp. 881–5.
20. Ibid., Book XII, ch. 9, 1074b34, p. 885.
21. Aristotle, *Ethics*, Book I, ch. 7, 1097b, trans. J.A.K. Thomson, Harmondsworth: Penguin, 1987, p. 74, where the phrase is translated as 'social being'.
22. Ibid., Book I, ch. 5, 1095b, p. 68.
23. Ibid., Book I, ch. 5, 1097b, p. 74.
24. Ibid., Book II, ch. 1, 1103b, p. 91.
25. Ibid., Book II, ch. 7, 1107b, p. 103.
26. See the Friends of Herculaneum Society website: www.herculaneum.ox.ac.uk for more on the Villa of the Papyri and the preserved scrolls.
27. Diogenes Laertius, *Lives and Opinions of Eminent Philosophers*, Vol. I, Book I, Prologue, §16, p. 17.
28. Edward Gibbon (1776), *The Decline and Fall of the Roman Empire*, London: J.M. Dent, 1962, Vol. IV, ch. XXXVII, p.8. Referring to the monasteries, he writes:
   The affrighted provincials of every rank, who fled before the barbarians, found shelter and subsistence; whole legions were buried in these religious sanctuaries.

29. Ancius Boethius (c.524 CE), *The Consolations of Philosophy*, Harmondsworth: Penguin, 1976.
30. Xenophon, *Conversations of Socrates*, London: Penguin, 1990, p. 126.
31. Thucydides, *History of the Peloponnesian War*, Harmondsworth: Penguin, 1984, pp. 144–51.
32. See, for instance, A.E. Taylor (1926), *Plato: The Man and his Work*, London: Methuen, 1966, p. 42.
33. Diogenes Laertius, *Lives and Opinions of Eminent Philosophers*, Vol. II, Book VI, Ch. 7, Hipparchia, §96, p. 99.

1.3 Medieval Philosophy

> In the Middle Ages the demarcation of the sphere of religious thought and that of worldly concerns was nearly obliterated . . . All life was saturated with religion to such an extent that the people were in constant danger of losing sight of the distinction between things spiritual and things temporal. If, on the one hand, all details of ordinary life may be raised to a sacred level, on the other hand, all that is holy sinks to the commonplace, by the fact of being blended with everyday life.
>
> J. Huizinga, *The Waning of the Middle Ages* (1924)[1]

Thanks to the triumph of religious bigotry in reducing everything to matters of religion, philosophy played almost no role during the Dark Ages. During both the Dark Ages and the medieval period, Western Europe was dominated by the Church which was in a sense the multinational organisation of the time. Conventionally, the medieval period begins in 312 CE with the conversion of the Emperor Constantine to Christianity and ends in the 1520s with Luther and the Reformation.[2] This overlooks the extent to which philosophy, general learning and scientific curiosity were eclipsed during the period 550 CE to 800 CE, which were the Dark Ages proper. As Father Copleston puts it: 'In the first centuries of the Christian era there was scarcely any philosophy in the modern sense, in the sense, that is, of an autonomous science distinct from theology.'[3]

The Christian Theologians
Augustine (354 – 430 CE)

As a philosopher, Augustine's principal concern was to reconcile Platonic philosophy with Christian doctrine. This makes him more of a theologian than a philosopher in the Greek tradition. He gave Christianity an immensely strong philosophical base which ensured its triumph over all its opponents and its ultimate takeover of the Roman Empire. As John Lewis puts it:

> Augustine gave to the Church a conception of predestination and irresistible grace which was really a form of religious determinism. This gave to Christian men a tremendous feeling of their strength

and authority in the world. Men who are possessed with the idea that they are predestined instruments in the hands of God have effected more than those who have believed themselves to be entirely free agents. The role that the Church was to play during the Dark Ages, the conviction that it had the right to bind and lose not only spiritual things but earthly and worldly things, and therefore the right to subdue kings and emperors, was largely due to this belief that it was the irresistible instrument of the Divine Will.

No other single Christian thinker after St. Paul was to influence so profoundly the Christianity of western European peoples. Augustine possessed an acute and disciplined intellect; he was familiar with the best Roman thought and with contemporary Greek philosophy. He was no mean orator and a great organiser. His thought dominated Christianity for 800 years.[4]

Augustine thought that the Christian philosopher's twofold role is to seek knowledge (1) of the nature of God and (2) of his own soul, the human self. He took the Platonic view that the soul is not the entire man but his better part, so that the body is a prison for the soul and a mark of man's fallen state. One important consequence is the emphasis he put on freewill. As the seat of the will is reason, when people exercise their will, they are acting in the image of God, the supreme rational being. This not only makes gods of us all but also makes the pursuit of godliness the sole end of our lives, as opposed to the philosophical pursuit of truth and knowledge for their own sakes. The latter view disappears from western thinking virtually till the scientific revolution of the seventeenth century.

Augustine also argued against the sceptical philosophy of Plato's academy by saying that the fact that we can be deceived makes it certain that we exist. Like Descartes, Augustine puts the point in the first person, 'If I am deceived, then I exist' (*Si fallor, sum*). A variation on this occurs in *On the Trinity,* where he says that if he is deceived, he is at least certain that he is alive. This refutation of scepticism made it increasingly unfashionable to be sceptical of one's beliefs. Anyone who did not believe absolutely in the tenets of Christianity was regarded with suspicion. The triumph of these views was responsible for stifling philosophical debate for centuries, that is to say, during the Dark Ages.

Augustine's most enduring work is his *Confessions.* This is sometimes said to be the first autobiography but he is really concerned to bare his soul to God and confess his sins. He sometimes lapses into absurdity as when he spends five or six pages being remorseful about his theft of pears at the age of fifteen. However, there are important philosophical passages in this book. For instance, there are some timeless passages on the subject of time. 'What then is time? I know well enough what it is, provided that no one asks me; but if I am asked what it is and try to explain, I am baffled.'[5] What he says about time is still relevant to

The revival of philosophy and learning

Learning began to revive from the reign of Charlemagne (742–814) onwards, with the so-called Carolingian Renaissance. This was possibly spurred on by the influence and rivalry of the Iberian Muslims. Though Charlemagne was brought up illiterate, he tried hard to overcome his failings and he encouraged and patronised learned men such as the English scholar Alcuin (735–804). Christianity thereafter became part of the fabric of a developing society, and gradually ceased to undermine that fabric by being the be-all and end-all of people's existence.

arguments about time today. Also, his remarks on language development[6] are used by Wittgenstein at the beginning of his book, *Philosophical Investigations*. In short, Augustine was the prime philosopher of Christianity to whom Protestants later reverted for their philosophy during the Reformation in the sixteenth century.

Aquinas (1225–1274)

Aquinas was Italian by birth and a son of the Count of Aquino. He was fortunate enough to study at the University of Paris under Albert the Great who was a formidable theologian in his own right. He also benefited from the vogue for Aristotelian studies during his lifetime. He wrote a formidable series of books on theology, some books countering the prevailing opinions of his fellow theologians, and a series of commentaries on Aristotle's works.

Aquinas was a theologian who used philosophy in the service of his theological arguments. He wrote very clearly and exhaustively about an extremely difficult subject. He aimed to show how theology benefited from philosophical argumentation, especially that of Aristotle, whom he regarded as 'The Philosopher'. In works such as the *Summa Theologica* he scrupulously and methodically gives the arguments both for and against every question which he raises. He was therefore extremely talented at using logical arguments in a straightforward, step-by-step way before arriving at his own conclusions.

He was insightful in his use of Aristotle's philosophy to bolster Christianity and his own belief in God. His theological writings contain fascinating insights into the nature of divine and angelic intellects. (His honorific title was 'Doctor Angelicus'.) He imagines what an incorporeal, immaterial being such as an angel would be like. To our modern minds, such insights are highly speculative and ultimately belong to the realms of science fiction.

He became extremely fashionable after his death and his philosophy ultimately became the official philosophy of the Roman Catholic Church. Aquinas's influence is still evident today. Many Catholic intellectuals such as Frederick Copleston (author of *A History of Philosophy*) regard his philosophy as canonical.

His view was limited because he was unable or unwilling to question the authority of Aristotle except to clarify or develop some points of detail. His attempt to reconcile Aristotle with Christianity was bound to fail because Aristotle had a scientific outlook that is ultimately incompatible with absolute religious belief.

Duns Scotus (1266–1308)

> *'Scotia me genuit, Anglia me suscepit, Gallia me docuit, Colonia me tenet'*
> Scotland begot me, England reared me, France taught me, Cologne holds my remains.[6]

Duns Scotus was a master of the medieval disputation. This form of disputation consists in the posing of questions and answering them, usually before a large audience of fellow disputants. This led him to make very subtle and profound arguments. He was therefore justly known as 'Doctor Subtilis'– the subtle doctor. He was in the thick of thirteenth- and fourteenth-century theological controversies which led up to the Renaissance. He was a diligent disputant of his predecessors but he does not appear to have developed his views as systematically as Aquinas. However, the extent of his works is not known for certain.

His chief insight was into the nature of individuation. He held that a thing gets its individuality by which we distinguish it from other things through its 'singularity' (*haecceitas* or 'thisness'). Our idea of a thing includes its existence in space and time as well as its qualities of colour, texture and shape. He was arguing against Aquinas who thought that things could only really be known by divine or angelic intellects. In other words, Duns Scotus was laying the foundations for scientific knowledge of physical objects.

Duns Scotus was fashionable for a time before Aquinas became ascendant. He was very much a transitional figure between the extreme theological doctrinists and the more openminded approach which preceded the Renaissance. He influenced subsequent thinkers such as William of Ockham (*c.*1295–1347). When the philosophy of Aquinas became the orthodox view, those who opposed that view became known as 'dunces'. As Duns Scotus failed to develop his views as systematically and voluminously as Aquinas, his views were inevitably less influential than those of Aquinas.

//

Arguments for the Existence of God

Philosophical arguments for the existence for God began in earnest with Aristotle's *Metaphysics*, as already discussed. Cicero's *The Nature of the Gods* contains the classic 'natural theology' account of God as creator and caretaker of the universe. The following is a summary of the arguments for the existence of God which have emerged from the medieval period. (For the latest statement of such arguments, see chapter three of Richard Dawkins' *The God Delusion* (2006).)

Ontological argument

This argument was first formulated by St Anselm (1033–1109) and it states that a perfect being must exist by definition. It uses logic to demonstrate beyond doubt the existence of God. We contradict ourselves if we think of a perfect being existing only in thought but not in reality. A perfect being would not be perfect if it lacked the attribute of real existence. No greater or more perfect being can exist than the one that exists absolutely. Thus, an unsurpassably perfect being must exist otherwise it would not be unsurpassably perfect. No matter how logically persuasive this argument may be, it still means that God exists only in our minds and in our thinking of him and not because there is concrete evidence of his existence. The ontological argument was later taken up and developed by Descartes in his *Meditations*.

Design (or teleological) argument

This is the most ancient and venerable argument for the existence of God and is implied throughout the Old Testament. If God created the world then we would expect all things on it to be designed and to fulfil God's purposes in their design. Therefore, God must exist because we find that indeed the world is purposeful and that only a divine designer could make the intricate and complex things that we see in nature. Just as man-made artefacts are designed, therefore so must natural objects have a designer.

First cause (or cosmological) argument

This argument states that as every event is caused by a prior event, therefore an original cause is required to start the process. There is change in the world, and change is always the effect of some cause or causes. Each cause is itself the effect of a further cause or set of causes; this chain moves in a series that either never ends or is completed by a first cause, which must be of a radically different nature in that it is not itself caused. Such a first cause is an important aspect, though not the entirety, of what Christianity means by God.

Miracles and visions argument

This argument states that the occurrence of miracles and visions proves that God must exist. Often the strength of people's personal experiences and inner certainty are sufficient for them to be convinced of the existence of God. They are therefore motivated to believe in the potency of alleged miracles and visions even though the evidence in favour of their reality may not be strong.

Moral argument

This presumes that moral conduct is impossible unless there is a God standing over us to ensure that we behave ourselves. Anything is permissible if there isn't a God to bolster our conscience and make us guilty and ashamed when we misbehave or fail to fulfil our obligations. But it can be argued that all moral behaviour results from social conditioning and upbringing. An external monitor is not required. Therefore, moral arguments for divine existence are not strictly provable.

Pascal's wager

Blaise Pascal (1623–1662), the French mathematician and thinker, formulated this argument in his *Pensées* published after his death.[8] It is an argument not so much for the existence of God as for a belief in God's existence. By believing in God, you can hedge your bets just in case there is in fact a God. Reason cannot decide whether there is or is not a God. Therefore we have nothing to lose by believing in God even though we are not entirely convinced of his existence. The possible rewards for believing make it worthwhile to take a chance and believe notwithstanding our doubts. If it turns out that God does exist, we will get our reward in heaven. If he does not exist, and death is total annihilation then we have lost nothing. But if we continue to disbelieve and we are proved to be wrong then we face a hell of torment. Pascal's wager therefore provides motivating and prudential reasons for believing in God, rather than one based on evidence. But it is surely unworthy of the majesty of God for us to believe in him for such base and selfish reasons.

The onset of the Renaissance

During the Middle Ages, as we have seen, interest in philosophy remained theological, namely, the use of logic and metaphysics to prove the existence of God, to solve the problem of why he allowed evil to persist in the world, and to face similar theological problems. Aristotle was the main man as far as the medieval philosophers were concerned. He was, as Dante put it, *Il maestro di color che sanno* – 'the master of those who know'. 'Those who know' included Socrates and Plato.[9] Only with the Renaissance, did interest in philosophy increase and broaden. The fall of Constantinople in 1453 brought about a great influx of scholars and their libraries into Western Europe. As a result, learning and philosophy became very fashionable among the aristocracy, especially in Italy.

Marsillio Ficino (1433–1499) translated Plato's dialogues into Latin and this brought Plato to scholars' attention. Ficino was a cleric who became a canon of Florence cathedral. He was appointed by Cosimo de' Medici as President of an academy for the study of Platonic doctrines. Ficino considered these doctrines to be a confirmation of Christianity and he was responsible for the expression 'Platonic love', which he coined in translating Plato's *Symposium* into Latin.

Pico della Mirandola (1463–1494) exemplifies the humanism that also became fashionable with his work *De Hominis Dignitate* – Of The Dignity of Man.

Niccolò di Bernardo dei Machiavelli (1469–1527) went beyond a humanistic view to concentrate too much on human failings. As a result, his famous book, *The Prince*, argues that all means of establishing and maintaining the authority of the state by the worst acts of the ruler are justified because of the wickedness and treachery of the governed.

Michel de Montaigne (1533–1592) wrote *Essays* which tell us in explicit terms what he is like as a human being, warts and all. With his work, the movement of the Renaissance from excessive religiosity and towards openminded humanism reached its acme.

Notes

1. J. Huizinga (1924), *The Waning of the Middle Ages*, Harmondsworth: Penguin, 1955, ch. XII, pp. 157–8.
2. Cf. David Luscombe (1997), *Medieval Thought*, Oxford: Oxford University Press, 1997, p. 2.
3. Frederick Copleston, SJ (1950), *A History of Philosophy*, New York: Image Books, 1962, Vol. 2, Part 2, p. 275.
4. John Lewis (1970), *History of Philosophy*, London: English Universities Press, 1970, p. 71.
5. Augustine, *Confessions*, trans. R.S. Pine-Coffin, Harmondsworth: Penguin, 1968, Book XI, 14, p. 264.
6. Ibid., Book I, 8, p. 29.
7. The epitaph of Duns Scotus on his tomb in the Conventual Franciscan church in Cologne. Cf. William A. Frank and Allan B. Wolter (1995), *Duns Scotus, Metaphysician*, West Lafayette, Indiana: Purdoe University Press, 1995, p. 1.
8. Blaise Pascal (1662), *Pensées*, trans. A.J. Krailsheimer, Harmondsworth: Penguin, 1975, Series II, §418, pp. 150–53.
9. Dante Alighieri (c.1321), *The Divine Comedy*, trans. Dorothy L. Sayers, Harmondsworth: Penguin, 1976, Hell (*L'Inferno*), Canto IV, 130–35.

1.4 Seventeenth-Century Philosophy

In the Renaissance, we can trace the beginnings of a human self-assertion against the world. We can see humanity shaking itself out of sleep and awakening to the possibility of escaping from the old tradition of submission to fate. This led to a growing preoccupation with the material world, since control of conditions means first and foremost the power to use the material of the world for human purposes. The condition of such control is understanding. Science arose as the effort to understand the material world in order to dominate it and use it.

John Macmurray, *Interpreting the Universe* (1936)[1]

The modern world, with its continuous development of scientific knowledge and technological achievement, was presaged by Renaissance humanism and self-confidence. But it began in real earnest during the seventeenth century. The Renaissance prepared the way by opening men's minds to their own capabilities which had previously been hampered by religious humility and deference to divinity. The apostle, so to speak, of this modern movement was Francis Bacon who laid down the principles which made possible the seventeenth-century scientific revolution.

Francis Bacon (1561–1626)

Bacon learnt from the Renaissance reaction against scholastic philosophy and against Aristotle in particular, and went well beyond it. He changed everything by laying the foundations for the scientific revolution of the seventeenth century with his pivotal work, *Novum Organon* (1620). Instead of the logical deduction laid down in Aristotle's *Organon*, Bacon stressed the importance of induction by which we arrive at theories from observation and experiment. He condemned both Plato and Aristotle. Truth was not an abstract, eternal thing as Plato taught. It comes from without by constant observation and experiment. Bacon said: 'When philosophy is severed from its roots in experience, it becomes a dead thing.' Philosophy consists in doing things and not in holding opinions:

> Of myself I say nothing; but in behalf of the business which is in hand I entreat men to believe that it is not an opinion to be held, but a work to be done; and to be well assured that I am labouring to lay the foundation, not of a sect or doctrine, but of human utility and power.[2]

Bacon was therefore concerned not with abstract truth but with mastery over nature. He eschewed logical deductions from untested first principles in favour of interrogating nature to change the world for the better. He was 'a trumpeter, not a combatant' and his trumpeting was not to summon men to battle but 'to make peace between themselves' and turn their united forces against the Nature of Things and 'extend the bounds of human empire' within their God-given limitations.[3]

He stressed the importance of doubt: 'If a man will begin with certainties, he shall end in doubt; but if he will be content to begin in doubt he shall end in certainties.' Thus, the intellectualistic approach, that is, the use of reason for its own sake, leads to scepticism. This occurs when we follow the Aristotelian 'contemplative life' to excess in an ascetic manner. Whatever you can know will be shown by what you can do. Philosophy enables us to use our understanding to act on nature and make things better, showing us that the life is not a vale of tears, but a vista replete with opportunities.

Bacon was thus advocating a dualistic interaction between ourselves and nature, and between the intellect and the practical aspects of our nature. He was the first to clarify the distinction between empiricism and rationalism, and he reconciled these opposing tendencies by advocating a dualist, trial-and-error procedure:

> Those who have treated the sciences were either empiricists or rationalists. Empiricists are like ants; they collect and put to use; but rationalists, like spiders, spin threads out of themselves. The bee takes the middle way, gathering her material from flowers in gardens and fields, and then digesting and transforming it using her own skills. Similarly, the true role of philosophy lies neither in relying entirely on the mental faculties nor in accumulating data in the memory from natural history or mechanical experiments, but in changing and reworking the material in the intellect. Therefore, we have good reason for hope from a closer and stricter union between the experimental and rational faculties than was the case before.[4]

We should therefore rely not entirely on knowledge gathered from our immediate experience of things nor entirely on knowledge deduced from our thinking about things. We should use both these processes in an interactive, trial-and-error way. However, Bacon did not develop fully in a philosophical way the cumulative dualism implied in the above passage. He left it to Descartes to advocate a much less satisfactory form of dualism which allowed empiricism and rationalism to go their separate ways. Science retained its interactive, growth potential and gradually established itself as a distinct subject from philosophy, which became bogged down in the quagmire of empiricist/rationalist factions. The resultant phenomenal success of science eventually led many philosophers to lose confidence in philosophy as having a different role to play from that played by science.

///

Empiricism

- Knowledge is derived from experience and ultimately from the senses.

- The mind is a blank sheet on which our ideas are written through our experience of the world. There are no innate ideas.

- At its extreme, empiricism leads to piecemeal heaps and collections of things as they are directly experienced. Any ordering of our experiences is considered to be arbitrary and unrealistic.

Rationalism

- Knowledge is deduced from reasoning or thinking about things.

- Perceptual experience is not enough to account for our understanding of things and *a priori* knowledge is not reducible to sensory information.

- At its extreme, everything is explained ultimately in relation to a single system of thought which constitutes 'reality'. Everything is amenable to reason.

\\\

The Early Rationalists

René Descartes (1596–1650)

Descartes is known as 'the founder' and even 'the father of modern philosophy'. But he was really an instigator of the profound division between rationalists and empiricists. Philosophy thereafter became distinct from 'natural philosophy' which went its own way as a purposeful truth-seeking community while philosophy continued to be sect-oriented and prone to fashionable excesses.

Descartes attempted to account for the scientific and mathematical advances of the seventeenth century with a clear and systematic philosophy that has been argued about ever since. His philosophy of ideas was basically rationalistic since he championed the cause of human reason as a means of overcoming scepticism. But he failed to reconcile his rationalism with the empiricist view that is also essential to science. He laid out his philosophy in two remarkably short books, *Discourse on Method* (1637) and *Meditations on the First Philosophy* (1641). As a philosopher, he did a lot more thinking than he did writing. In his *Meditations*, he imagines that he is being deceived by an 'evil demon'. The following remarkable passage presages the scientific fiction of films such as *The Matrix* and the idea that we may be nothing but 'brains in a vat':

> I shall suppose, therefore, that there is, not a true God, who is the sovereign source of truth, but some evil demon, no less cunning and deceiving than powerful, who has used all his artifice to deceive me. I will suppose that the heavens, the air, the earth, colours, shapes, sounds and all external things that we see, are only illusions and deceptions which he uses to take me in. I will consider myself as having no hands, eyes, flesh, blood or senses, but as believing wrongly that I have all these things. I shall cling obstinately to this notion; and if, by this means, it is not in my power to arrive at the knowledge of any truth, at the very least it is in my power to suspend my judgement. This is why I shall take great care not to accept into my belief anything false, and shall so well prepare my mind against all the tricks of this great deceiver that, however powerful and cunning he may be, he will never be able to impose on me.[5]
>
> Let him deceive me who may, but he shall never be able to cause me to be nothing, so long as I think that I am something.[6]

From these arguments, Descartes gets his *cogito, ergo sum*, 'I think therefore I am.' This is sometimes rendered as 'I am thinking therefore I am' or 'I doubt therefore I am.' Thus it is by self-conscious activity in our minds that we establish our existence as distinct entities.

On the one hand, he said: 'I easily persuaded myself that I had no idea in my mind which had not passed beforehand through my senses.'[7] This is the source of the empiricist view that all our ideas are derived from sensory experience and that truth must be verified in relation to that experience. On the other hand, he mistrusted the immediacy of the senses, for example, when we look at the sun, we see a small disc in the sky whereas we know that in reality it is an unimaginably huge object many times the size of our planet. So, Descartes said:

> This teaches me ever to conclude from these diverse perceptions of the senses, anything concerning external things, without the mind having carefully and maturely examined them. For it is, it seems to me, the function of the mind alone, and not of the composition of mind and body, to know the truth of these things.[8]

This is the source of the rationalist view that only by reasoning about things can we reach the truth of things. It is either all out there or all in the mind.

He then argues that all our ideas are in our minds so that our minds are distinct not only from the objects of perception but also our bodies. He thinks that the mind and body are separate substances and this is the source of Cartesian dualism. The mind 'is a thinking thing, and not extended in length, breadth and depth, and does not participate in anything that pertains to the body'.[9] The great problem with this view is that the mind is totally distinct from the body and their interrelationship remains mysterious and inexplicable. It thus fails to account adequately for the relation between mind and body. This failure has generally discredited the dualist view up to the present day.

However, Cartesian dualism is a very limited form of dualism that makes absolute distinctions between mind and body, mental and physical, and subject and object, as if these were distinct objects or substances. A theory of interactive dualism is possible which accounts in detail for the way we interact constantly with whatever is external to us. Our apprehension of reality is then the result of this constant feedback process which all too often grinds to halt thus making us authoritarian, unreasonable or plain mad.

Benedict de Spinoza (1632–1677)

Like Descartes, Spinoza is also in the tradition of Continental rationalism. He is renowned not only for his rigorous attempt to prove the existence of God by geometrical demonstration but, more importantly, for his belief in the power of human reason. He was a pantheist who believed that God is to be found everywhere in the universe. He argued that only one substance exists and that is *deus sive natura* – God or nature. He treats this as self-evident and deduces his 'ethics' from it. Thus, like Parmenides, Spinoza thought that everything in the universe is One. This one substance has an infinite number of attributes but, as we are finite beings, we can only conceive of two attributes: extension and thought. While Descartes regarded mind and body as separate substances, Spinoza argued that mind and body are merely different ways of thinking about the same reality which is God or nature. This reality is entirely self-contained, self-causing and self-sufficient. Everything in the universe is a part of God and everything that happens is a necessary part of the divine nature. God is the cause of all things but only within the universe and not outside it. This is not a personal God but a rational construct. Spinoza was rightly called 'a God-intoxicated man'.

Like Aristotle, Spinoza did not look for moral principles outside man or seek the good in itself. Every man should seek what is truly useful to him; but in the long run what he seeks, is knowledge and perfect understanding. To be blessed is to have the contentment of Spirit that arises from knowledge of God (i.e. of Reality). Since men necessarily seek their own preservation and the indefinite extension of their power and liberty, this is the starting point of an inquiry into society and politics. Social organisation comes into being because in perfecting his being nothing is more useful to man than man. 'Man is a God to man' since our power increases as we move towards a co-operation that joins it to the power of other men.[10] Our power is the virtue within us that expresses our inner nature which is God-given. Thus, even social activity is ultimately determined by the nature of God.

Though Spinoza was a determinist, he thought that we have freewill in exercising our intellect. Through reason we can control our emotions and become rational beings:

> He therefore who moderates his emotions and desires from a love of freedom – he, I say, endeavours as much as possible to obtain a knowledge of the virtues and their causes, and to fill his mind with that joy which arises from a true knowledge of them, and by no means to regard the vices of men, to disparage his fellows and rejoice in a false species of liberty – will be able in a short space of time to direct his actions for the most part according to the direction of reason.[11]

Spinoza's geometrical way of arguing with 'propositions' and 'proofs' was used during the eighteenth century by Newtonian theologians such as Samuel Clarke (1675–1729) who attempted to prove the necessary existence of God even more rigorously than Spinoza. It was also used by Giambattista Vico in his *Scienza Nuova* (1744). More importantly, Hegel was influenced greatly by Spinoza in constructing his own version of pantheism. Spinoza's holistic method unified everything in one truthful system. Each proposition coheres with every other proposition. It is therefore the rationalist model of truth as coherence which has been used particularly by continental philosophers up to the present day. The idea of truth corresponding to external realities was left to empiricist philosophers, as we shall see.

Gottfried Wilhelm von Leibniz (1646–1716)

Leibniz was not only a great philosopher and mathematician but also a skilled diplomat – a very worldly philosopher, contrasting with the unworldly nature of his philosophy. He developed the rationalist view in a thoroughly metaphysical way. His metaphysics was so elaborate and divorced from empirical realities that Kant used it as the model of 'pure reason' which he attacked in his *Critique of Pure Reason*.

Leibniz made an important distinction between truths of reason which he called 'necessary', and truths of fact which he called 'contingent'. The opposite of a necessary truth is impossible but the opposite of a contingent truth is possible. The reason for a truth being necessary can be found by analysis, 'that is, by resolving it into simpler ideas and truths until the primary ones are reached'.[12] If someone says, 'I have a wife though I am unmarried', we immediately know that statement to be untrue because having a wife necessarily means being married. If it is said that marriage means having children, we can see that this can only be contingently true because it is possible to be married without having children. This necessary/contingent distinction is important because Kant later developed it further in his *Critique* by relating it to the distinctions: analytic/synthetic and *a priori/a posteriori*.

Leibniz also formulated the Principle of Sufficient Reason: 'by virtue of which we consider that no fact can be real or existing and no proposition can be true unless there is a sufficient reason, why it should be thus and not otherwise, even though in most cases these reasons cannot be known by us'.[13] However, this principle is questionable in the way it is formulated by Leibniz. There is a sufficient reason for everything because we are rationalising beings who are very good at finding reasons for anything. We can invent reasons for our most absurd actions, for example, when we do absurd things under the influence of a hypnotist. But Leibniz formulates his principle in this limited way because it is part of his arguments for the existence of God. According to him, only God has access to the reasons for everything. But this anthropomorphic view of God makes him no more than a very knowledgeable being who is otherwise like us.

Monads are an important part of Leibniz's metaphysics. Monads – from the Greek *monas* 'unit' – are essentially units of consciousness. They are the idealist's answer to materialism and provide an alternative way of looking at the universe instead of regarding it as full of material atoms and energy fields. Monads are basic substances that make up the universe but lack spatial extension and hence are immaterial. Each monad is a unique, indestructible, dynamic, soul-like entity whose properties are a function of its perceptions and appetites. Monads have no true causal relations with other monads. They are all are perfectly synchronised with each other by God in a pre-established harmony. The objects of the material world are simply appearances of collections of monads. Since the monad of monads is God, this whole system is another set-up to bolster Leibniz's arguments for the existence of God. However, Kant later showed that the excessive use of reason by rationalists such as Leibniz and Spinoza leads to antinomies and paradoxes that are fatal to their arguments.

The English Empiricists

Thomas Hobbes (1588–1679)

As a young man, Hobbes was a close associate of Francis Bacon whom he helped with his writings and Latin translations of Bacon's essays. His somewhat turgid style of writing doubtless comes from Bacon's influence. However, Hobbes did not maintain Bacon's balance between empiricism and rationalism. In his later writings, he veered towards extreme empiricism and materialism. His passion for logic and geometry led him to rationalise human affairs but from an empirical point of view. He applies his own version of the geometric method in the

The origins of English empiricism

The idea that our knowledge is derived from experience is deeply rooted in the English psyche. It was embodied in the legal system based on precedents rather than on pre-conceived principles, especially the Roman legal principles on which Continental and Scottish law were based. The emphasis on freedom from tyranny laid down in Magna Carta ensured that central authority could not impose its will arbitrarily but must consult the people and learn by experience what can or cannot be done. Even the English scholastic philosophers tended towards the empirical view, the best example being Roger Bacon (c.1212–c.1292) who was interested in experimental science and the practical application of mathematics. William of Ockham (c.1295–1347) is famous for his 'razor' whereby 'entities are not to be multiplied beyond necessity'. This 'razor' is used to cut philosophical and scientific theories to the bone and achieve simplicity in place of incomprehensible complexity. Ockham was also a nominalist who held that only particular objects exist. General words such as redness, man, butter or species don't exist as real things independently of the particular things that exemplify their use. This empiricist view holds that words are related to reality by our use and experience of them. They are not real in the way implied by Plato's theory of forms. Not surprisingly, Hobbes and Locke were nominalists. English empiricism therefore reflects the anti-authoritarian tendency in English history, just as rationalism reflects Continental authoritarian attitudes derived originally from the Roman Empire and perpetuated by the Roman Catholic Church.

Leviathan (1651), but unlike Spinoza his empiricism leads him to sceptical conclusions and a notoriously pessimistic view of human nature.

In typical empiricist fashion he begins his *Leviathan* with a chapter on perception concerning how objects cause themselves to be perceived. Thus, our knowledge is derived more from the material world than from our reasoning about it. According to Hobbes, man acts according to certain natural laws. Just as matter behaves rigidly according to physical laws unless acted upon, the natural state of man is to obey the laws of his aggressive, animal nature. His life is one of war and strife, unless acted upon and governed by the rules and laws of society. Only a covenant or 'social contract' enforced by the rule of the sword keeps man from falling back into his natural state. We contract away some of our rights in exchange for the security that strong government and the law give us against our enemies. Without this covenant, society inevitably reverts to its natural state of war in which 'every man is enemy to every man' and the life of man becomes 'solitary, poor, nasty, brutish and short'.[14]

Hobbes applied his materialism unremittingly. He thought that everything in the universe is corporeal and there are no such things as incorporeal spirits or souls. All mentions of 'spirit' in the Bible refer 'either to a subtile, fluid, and invisible Body, or a Ghost, or other Idol or Phantasme of the Imagination'. It may also be a metaphor for something else material.[15] Even God is mere matter since he is not the creator of things but the 'irresistible power' of nature. We are punished for our sins because we infringe the laws of nature.[16] The word of God follows from 'the Dictates of reason and equity'.[17] But God is being identified not with Nature but with the material effects of Nature on us.

As this materialism is governed by laws of nature, it creates problems for the existence of freewill since everything material is causally determined. However, Hobbes argues that man is free as long as he acts in accordance with his nature, just as water is free in the way it flows randomly down a mountainside. Freedom consists not in the ability to do things but in the absence of opposition to do things.[18] This distinction gives us two kinds of freedom – negative freedom in which our freedom is not opposed, and positive freedom in which we are empowered to do things. This inspired an important philosophical essay on that subject by Isaiah Berlin, called 'Two Concepts of Liberty'.[19] Positive freedom leads to libertarian excesses such as the Reign of Terror and terrorism and tyranny in general. Hobbes's *Leviathan* is undoubtedly a work of genius in which he says many striking things such as the following:

> Words are wise men's counters; they do but reckon with them. But they are the money of fools, that value them by the authority of an *Aristotle*, a *Cicero*, or a *Thomas*, or any other Doctor whatsoever, if but a man.[20]

John Locke (1632–1704)

Locke's most enduring philosophical work is his *Essay Concerning Human Understanding* (1689), which lays down the principles of empiricist philosophy more thoroughly than was attempted by Hobbes. Its programme of working out a science of human nature culminated in the science of psychology by the middle of the nineteenth century. Locke argues that all our ideas are derived from perception and he calls this 'my new way of knowing by means of ideas'.[21] He therefore begins his book by arguing against Descartes' assumption that some of our ideas are innate. Such logical principles as 'whatever is, is' and 'it is impossible for the same thing to be and not to be' are not universally assented to, let alone inborn. He also argues that our moral principles and our ideas of God and substance are not innate. Thereafter, he painstakingly works out what ideas are and how they relate to perceptions on the one hand and words on the other hand.

In his treatment of ideas, Locke makes an important distinction between primary and secondary ideas. The primary qualities of material object consist in their 'solidity, extension, figure, number and motion or rest', whereas their secondary qualities include 'colours, sounds, smells, tastes' and other 'sensible qualities'.[22] He then shows how our simple ideas derived from the senses are built up into complex ideas from which we get our ideas of substances such as wood, birds and so on. The whole of Book III, 'Of Words', is devoted to showing how we name substances and the problems that words give us. Book IV, 'Of

Knowledge', concerns the nature of knowledge and the extent to which we can or cannot rely on it. Our knowledge is no more reliable than the ideas on which it is based. He also deals with our reasoning powers and the following passage shows his scepticism of the value of Aristotelian logic:

> But God has not been so sparing to men to make them barely two-legged creatures, and left it to *Aristotle* to make them rational . . . God has been more bountiful to mankind than so. He has given them a mind that can reason without being instructed in the methods of syllogising: the understanding is not taught to reason by these rules; it has a native faculty to perceive the coherence, or incoherence of its ideas, and can range them right, without any such perplexing repetitions. I say not this any way to lessen Aristotle, whom I look on as one of the greatest men amongst the antients; whose large views, acuteness and penetration of thought, and strength of judgment, few have equalled: and who in this very invention of forms of argumentation, wherein the conclusion may be shewn to be rightly inferred, did great service against those, who were not ashamed to deny any thing. And I readily own, that all right reasoning may be reduced to his forms of syllogism. But yet I think without any diminution to him I may truly say, that they are not the only, nor the best way of reasoning . . . .
>
> Tell a country gentlewoman, that the wind is south-west, and the weather louring, and like to rain, and she will easily understand, 'tis not safe for her to go abroad thin clad, in such a day, after a fever: she clearly sees the probable connexion of all these, without tying them together in those artificial and cumbersome fetters of several syllogisms, that clog and hinder the mind.[23]

Locke's political philosophy has also been very influential as laid out in his *Two Treatises of Civil Government* (1690). His view of society and the social contract is noticeably more benign than that of Hobbes in the *Leviathan*. Accordingly to Locke, the law of nature teaches us that 'all mankind who will but consult it, that being all equal and independent, no one ought to harm another in his life, health, liberty or possessions'.[24] This passage obviously influenced the American Declaration of Independence in its concern for the equality of men and 'the inalienable rights' of 'life, liberty and the pursuit of happiness'.

Notes

1. John Macmurray (1936), *Interpreting the Universe*, New York: Humanity Books, 1996, p. 83.
2. Francis Bacon (1623), *De Augmentis Scientiarum*, Book 4, ch. I.
3. Francis Bacon (1620), Preface to *The Great Instauration*. Kant quotes the Latin version of this preface at the beginning of his *Critique of Pure Reason*, as does Fichte at the beginning of his

Preface to the *Wissenschaftslehre* (Science of Knowledge).

4. Francis Bacon (1620), *Novum Organum*, First Book, aphorism 95.
5. René Descartes (1637/1641), *Discourse on Method* and *Meditations on the First Philosophy*, Harmondsworth: Penguin, 1968, First Meditation, p. 100.
6. Ibid., Second Meditation, pp. 114–15.
7. Ibid., Sixth Meditation, p. 154.
8. Ibid., Sixth Meditation, p. 161.
9. Ibid., Fourth Meditation, p. 132.
10. Benedict de Spinoza (1677), *Ethics*, London: J.M. Dent, 1970, Fourth Part, Prop. XXXV, Note, p. 164.
11. Ibid., Fifth Part, Prop. X, Note, p. 208.
12. G.W. Leibniz (1714), *Monadology*, §33, as in *Philosophical* Writings, London: J.M. Dent, 1990, p. 184.
13. Ibid., §32, p. 184.
14. Thomas Hobbes (1651), *Leviathan*, Harmondsworth: Penguin, 1985, Part I, ch. 13, p. 186.
15. Ibid., Part III, ch. 34, pp. 429–30.
16. Ibid., Part II, ch. 31, p. 397.
17. Ibid., Part III, ch. 36, p. 456.
18. Ibid., Part II, ch. 21, pp. 261–2.
19. Isaiah Berlin (1958), 'Two Concepts of Liberty', in *Political Philosophy*, ed. Anthony Quinton, Oxford: Oxford University Press, 1973, pp. 141–2.
20. Hobbes (1651), *Leviathan*, Part I, ch. 4, p. 106.
21. John Locke (1697), *Second Letter to Edward Stillingfleet, Bishop of Worcester*, p. 72. As quoted by A.C. Campbell in the 'Prolegomena' to his edition of Locke's *Essay* (1891), New York: Dover, 1959, pp. lix–lx. Actually, it was Stillingfleet who first pejoratively referred to 'this new way of ideas' and Locke turned the tables by making a virtue of it.
22. John Locke (1700 edn), *An Essay Concerning Human Understanding*, ed. P.H. Nidditch, Oxford: Clarendon Press, 1988, Book II, Ch.VIII, §22, p. 140.
23. Ibid., Book IV, Ch. XVII, §4, pp. 671–2.
24. John Locke (1690), *Two Treatises of Civil Government*, London: J.M. Dent (Everyman), 1970, Book II, Ch. II, §6, p. 119.

1.5 Eighteenth-Century Philosophy

> The passion for philosophy, like that for religion, seems liable to this inconvenience, that, though it aims at the correction of our manners, and the extirpation of our vices, it may only serve, by imprudent management, to push the mind, with more determined resolution, towards that side which already draws too much, by the bias of the natural temper.
>
> David Hume, *An Enquiry Concerning Human Understanding* (1772)[1]

The eighteenth century is famed for the great Enlightenment movement in philosophy which transformed the political landscape of Western Europe and beyond. The term 'Enlightenment' (*Aufklärung*) was first used by Kant in 1784, but the movement originates in seventeenth-century England with philosophers such as Bacon, Hobbes, Shaftesbury, Locke, Berkeley and Mandeville. 'Enlightenment' means creating the conditions for people to think for themselves – *sapere aude!* (dare to know!), as Kant put it.[2] In practice, it means championing human rights, freedom of speech, openmindedness and the questioning of authority. The Enlightenment progressed also because of a series of philosophers who challenged each other concerning the truth of their various assertions. Thus, we begin with the challenge made by Berkeley to Locke's empiricist excesses in making too much of the notion of 'idea'.

George Berkeley (1685–1753)

Berkeley found a fatal flaw in Locke's 'way of ideas' and produced an idealist, non-empiricist philosophy in answer to it. He realised that if our knowledge of the world is based on ideas then nothing really exists except these ideas. These ideas may enter our minds but there is no way of proving that these ideas refer to anything 'out there'. When we look at a building, we have the idea that it is a building but the idea itself is not enough for us to be absolutely sure that it is the building it appears to be. It may be, for example, a film-maker's cardboard replica, a dream or a hallucination. But Berkeley goes even further to argue that even if we satisfy ourselves beyond reasonable doubt that the building exists 'out there', it is still only a matter of our ideas. These ideas can't prove the independent existence of anything outside our thinking about them.

Berkeley was the first person to argue at length that everything is in the mind and nothing really exists outside our minds. Our ideas don't refer to the things themselves, therefore there can be no material world independent of these ideas and everything is happening in our minds. Our ideas of external objects are simply stronger and more vivid than those of our dreams or imagination. In support of that view, Berkeley disputed the existence of abstract, general ideas. For their existence would imply that some ideas are more real than others. Thus, he said that we can never have a general idea of a triangle but only of a particular one which is similar to other triangles. He asks how can there be a triangle 'which is neither oblique, nor rectangle, equilateral, equicrural, nor scalenon, but all and none of these at once?'[3] We can only have the idea of a particular triangle and not one that has all the features of triangles. But this is to misunderstand the nature of abstract concepts which are signs or symbols of things like numbers. Against Berkeley, it can be argued that these concepts exist only 'in the mind' but are used to make sense in an interactive way of what is independent of our minds.

Nevertheless, Berkeley reduced all ideas to the same level of reality to make an ideality, that is to say, a uniform, non-material existence which God is pleased to convey into our minds. He takes his argument to its logical conclusion by saying that nothing exists unless it is perceived. To him 'the absolute existence of unthinking things' without their being perceived, 'seems perfectly unintelligible. Their *esse* is *percipi*, nor is it possible they should have any existence, out of the minds or thinking things which perceive them.'[4] 'Consequently, so long as they are not actually perceived by me, or do not exist in my mind or that of any other created spirit, they must either have no existence at all, or else subsist in the mind of some Eternal Spirit.'[5] Hence, the two well-known limericks concerning the tree in the quad being observed by 'yours faithfully, God' when there is no else around to see them.

Berkeley also disputed Newton's view of absolute time and space. To that extent, he presaged the theory of relativity.[6] In his justly celebrated *Dialogues* (1713), he argues at great length that he is no sceptic and that he 'endeavours to vindicate common sense'.[7] His views never inspired a great following and his philosophy is generally regarded as an interesting curiosity which graphically shows the consequences of taking idealism to its logical conclusion. Later idealists such as Hegel strove hard not to be accused of Berkeleian idealism. Berkeley's philosophy was therefore important in that it forced later philosophers to be clearer about what ideas are and how our minds may or may not relate to external reality.

///

The Scottish Enlightenment

The Scottish Enlightenment added to the achievements of the English Enlightenment by working out the conditions for a civil society in which freedom is uppermost. It began after the union of the parliaments in 1707 when the Scots made a concerted effort to reach the cultural standards of the English. They established clubs and societies which were unique to Scotland in being exclusively dedicated to self-improvement in their behaviour, conversation and literary skills. These clubs were strictly disciplined with the use of rules and laws to ensure attendance and good behaviour. For example, the Easy Club was founded in 1712 by the poet Allan Ramsay (1685–1758, not his son, Allan Ramsay the artist). This club discussed and produced literature and poetry. Here is its eighth law:

> The Design of the Society being a Mutual Improvement of Minds by Conversation it is enacted that there be no gaming in the club or forcing one another to drink both being diverting from our great design and of times provoking to an undue exercise of the passions which is contrary to and inconsistent with our Commendable Easiness.[8]

These clubs and societies generated a general interest in philosophy and fostered writing of the highest quality and later made the Scottish writers very influential throughout Europe. Remarkably, the members of these early clubs were all in their teens and early twenties. Thus, the Fair Intellectual Club (1717), one of the few women's literary clubs that we know of, was restricted to ladies aged sixteen to twenty.[9] Intellectual improvement was 'cool' among these young people and they created the hothouse atmosphere for the next generation which included such geniuses as David Hume, Adam Smith, James Hutton, Robert Adam and Tobias Smollett. The subsequent popularity of philosophy in Scotland is exemplified by the following passage:

> It is well known that between 1723 and 1740, nothing was in more request with the Edinburgh *literati*, clerical and laical, than metaphysical disquisitions. These they regarded as more pleasant themes than either theological or political controversies, of which, by that time, people were surfeited. The writings of Locke and Clarke, of Butler and Berkeley, presented a wide and interesting field of inquiry, in which they could exercise their intellectual powers without endangering their own quiet and safety.[10]

Thus, the movement known as the Scottish Enlightenment was only possible because of the widespread popularity of philosophy and literature among educated people in Scotland during the eighteenth century.[11]

\\\

David Hume (1711–1776)

Hume is particularly famous because of the scale of his influence on subsequent philosophers. His writings influenced, for example, Thomas Reid's common sense philosophy, Kant's critical philosophy, Jeremy Bentham's utilitarianism and Adam Smith's ethics and economics. This is due to the rigour and depth of

Hume's arguments which make him very much a philosopher's philosopher. He attempted to create a science of human nature using Locke's empirical principles. He began assuming that all our perceptions 'resolve themselves into two distinct kinds' called impressions and ideas: '*Impressions*: All our lively and forceful sensations, passions and emotions. *Ideas*: Faint images of impressions in thinking and reasoning.'[12]

He then argues at length that any knowledge which cannot be traced back to impressions and ideas rooted in the senses must be doubtful if not false. This form of empirical reductionism was later challenged by Kant and the German idealists such as Hegel. It is arguable that the concept of chair transcends the perceptual appearances from which we build up that concept. It is more than just an amalgam of legs, colours, shapes or other parts of which it is composed. If it were not so then we could not use the concept to apply to objects that have none of the usual features of chairs. A chair's function is to be sat upon, and this is not a perceivable aspect of it. A pile of cushions on the floor can be sat upon and fulfil the chair's function but they don't look like one. The concept of a chair can therefore be extended to cushions without violating our usual image of a chair. Hume failed to appreciate that our concepts of things are more than perceptual images and that conception is not the same as imagination. This major flaw in his system of thought made him unduly sceptical of our reasoning powers, and it ensured that Humean empiricism cannot be reconciled with rationalism as it has the following extreme and mistaken consequences:

1. It leads to the well-known 'Hume's Fork' which weeds out all reasoning unless it is strictly 'abstract' or strictly 'experimental':

> If we take in our hand any volume; of divinity or school metaphysics, for instance; let us ask, *Does it contain any abstract reasoning concerning quantity or number?* No. *Does it contain any experimental reasoning concerning matter of fact and existence?* No. Commit it then to the flames: for it can contain nothing but sophistry and illusion.[13]

Hume was probably well aware that this 'fork' singles out his own philosophical works for burning. This unduly Draconian way of repudiating metaphysics was taken up enthusiastically by logical positivists in the twentieth century, though metaphysics is still very much alive and well.

2. The idea of the self vanishes when all our personal experiences are reduced to an endless succession of perceptions:

> When I enter most intimately into what I call *myself*, I always stumble upon some particular perception or other, or heat or cold,

light or shade, love or hatred, pain or pleasure. I can never catch *myself* at any time without a perception, and never can observe anything but the perception.[14]

Again we can counter this empiricist view by pointing out that we can have a concept of ourselves which is more than just a sum of successive perceptions. But Kant and the German idealists went to the other extreme and attributed the self or ego with transcendental powers which are more mysterious than elucidatory.

3. Our reliance on inductive reasoning is put in doubt. We can never be sure that the sun will rise tomorrow as presently unknown events may prevent it from doing so. We can only say that it is highly probable that the sun will rise tomorrow. But our deductive reasoning is just as doubtful and uncertain as our inductive reasoning. The uncertainty of logic and mathematics was shown in the twentieth century by Russell's Paradox and Gödel's Undecidability Theorem. What matters is not that our reasoning powers are limited and uncertain but that we know their limitations and use them strictly within their reliable limits, usually on a trial-and-error basis, which is how rocket science works.

4. According to Hume, our reasoning results from the connection or association of ideas. Thus, when one event is caused by another, we associate the ideas of the events because we have always done so in the past. This 'constant conjunction' between events explains the causal connection so that it is not necessarily real at all. In fact, it is not the case 'that the customary conjunction of objects determines their causation'.[15] When we assign causes to events we do so not out of habit but because we have reason to believe that a causal connection may be made. We have to think that a connection can be made and have a true or false reason such as a guess, evidence, theory or motive which explains the connection. The events remain isolated and singular occurrences in our minds unless our mental activity systematically connects the events in accordance with our conjectures, theories, laws or other explanations concerning about what is going on.

5. Hume's scepticism of our reasoning powers is carried into his ethical views. Thus, he famously said: 'Reason is, and ought only to be the slave of the passions, and can never pretend to any other office than to serve and obey them.'[16] But our reasoning powers are often needed to subdue our passions as when we stop being angry with someone when we realise that they are undeserving of our anger. Obeying the dictates of our emotions all the time is not only immoral but also impractical. Hume simply has too narrow a view of reason as being deductive, logical, syllogistic reasoning which, as Locke pointed out, is far from being all there is to our reasoning powers.

Hume devotes the whole of Book II of the *Treatise* (1739) to the 'passions'. This is an important but largely neglected part of the *Treatise*, in which he clearly outlines a dualistic account of how our passions or emotions oscillate from one extreme to another. In successive chapters he contrasts pride and humility, love and hatred, pleasure and pain, pity and envy and so on. However, Hume failed to make as much as he might have of the dualism implicit in this account of the passions. If he had developed this dualism instead of taking his empirical views to their logical conclusion, we might have been spared the subsequent polarisation of empiricism and rationalism which has characterised philosophy ever since.

Adam Smith (1723–1790)

Smith began as a disciple of Francis Hutcheson (1694–1746) and Shaftesbury (the third Earl, 1671–1713), and he was later influenced by his friendship with Hume. His ethics was part of the Enlightenment programme of showing that religious moral codes are not sufficient to produce mature and responsible persons taking their place in society. His main idea in ethics concerned the role of sympathy in our social interactions. He points out that we cannot approve or disapprove of our own behaviour unless and until we have learnt to approve or disapprove of the behaviour of other people. On the other hand, we judge others morally because we have learnt to compare our behaviour with theirs. We sympathise or fail to sympathise with other people's behaviour when we compare it with our own. Thus, our moral judgments cannot develop properly until we see ourselves as others see us:

> We can never survey our own sentiments and motives, we can never form any judgment concerning them, unless we remove our-selves, as it were, from our own natural station, and endeavour to view them as at a certain distance from us. But we can do this in no other way than by endeavouring to view them with the eyes of other people, or as other people are likely to view them.[17]

Our growing self-knowledge involves making ourselves aware of how others see us. We can do so interactively by dividing ourselves into (1) a 'fair and impartial spectator' judging our own conduct and (2) an agent whose actions are being judged impartially.[18] Unfortunately, Smith does not work out this dualistic view consistently as a metaphysical principle.

Smith's ethics at least improves on the religious view that we should submit ourselves entirely to the will of God regardless of the thoughts and feelings of our fellow beings. However, it can be taken to hypocritical extremes when we 'keep up appearances' so that we look better to others than we really are.

His ethics also fosters individual self-development on a 'live and let live' basis. We cannot develop 'self-command' or become good and dutiful citizens unless we work out for ourselves the best way to live. We must take responsibility for our own lives and not allow others to tell us how to live. A pursuit of self-interest, riches and the good things in life has unintended consequences in shaping society. Indeed, it benefits society as an 'invisible hand' which organises the distribution of available resources more evenly than otherwise:

> The rich . . . are led by an invisible hand to make nearly the same distribution of the necessaries of life which could have been made had the earth been divided into equal portions among all its inhabitants; and thus, without intending it, without knowing it, advance the interest of society, and afford means to the multiplication of the species.[19]

In later economic theory, the effect of such spending is known as 'the multiplier effect' whereby investment in buildings and manufactured goods stimulates the activity of the whole economy by increasing employment and the efficient use of resources. Thus, Smith's ethics is closely linked with the economic theory which he developed in his later *Wealth of Nations* book (1776) wherein the 'invisible hand' also appears:

> as every individual . . . . neither intends to promote the public interest, nor knows how much he is promoting it. By preferring the support of domestic to that of foreign industry, he intends only his own security; and by directing that industry in such as manner as its produce may be of the greatest value, he intends only his own gain, and he is in this, as in many other cases, led by an invisible hand to promote an end which was no part of his intention. By pursuing his own interest he frequently promotes that of the society more effectually than when he really intends to promote it.[20]

Previously, land and agriculture were thought to be the chief sources of a country's wealth, but Smith's book proved beyond doubt that its sources lie in industry, trade and commerce. He begins by showing the importance of specialisation or the division of labour, illustrated by the famous pin factory. Whereas one man by himself may make 1–20 pins a day, a factory with 10 skilled employees performing 18 distinct tasks could produce at least 48,000 pins per day.[21] He shows how the factors of production: capital, labour and land make industry work. But it is wrong to categorise Smith as a mere capitalist thinker. He put forward the labour theory of value which emphasised the value of the worker's contribution to an organisation's success. This theory was later used by Marx in his book on *Capital*. Smith also argued in favour of high wages:

> The liberal reward of labour, as it encourages the propagation, so it increases the industry of the common people. The wages of labour are the encouragement of industry, which, like every other human quality, improves in proportion to the encouragement it receives.[22]

He also draws attention to the importance of cost-cutting economies not only in increasing a company's efficiency and profitability but also in reducing the drudgery of working conditions:

> In the first steam-engines, a boy was constantly employed to open and shut alternately the communication between the boiler and the cylinder, according as the piston either ascended or descended. One of those boys, who loved to play with his companions, observed that, by tying a string from the handle of the valve which opened this communication to another part of the machine, the valve would open and shut without his assistance, and leave him at liberty to divert himself with his play-fellows. One of the greatest improvements that has been made upon this machine, since it was first invented, was in this manner the discovery of a boy who wanted to save his own labour.[23]

In short, Smith laid foundations for the science of economics, sound business practices and a political agenda, all of which brought about the Industrial Revolution without which the comforts of modern life would have been impossible. Undoubtedly, the careless application of his ideas created exploitation and bad working conditions. Also, his overemphasis on self-interest led to extreme individualism, the consequences of which are all too evident today. But the extremes to which philosopher's ideas are taken, are to be corrected by succeeding generations and not simply blamed on philosophers who are only doing their best with the ideas available to them.

Thomas Reid (1710–1796)

> It would be agreeable to fly to the moon, and to make a visit to Jupiter and Saturn; but when I know that Nature has bound me down by the law of gravitation to this planet which I inhabit, I rest contented, and quietly suffer myself to be carried along in its orbit.[24]

Reid began as a minister of the Kirk and eventually took Adam Smith's post at Glasgow University in1764. He was the founder of the Scottish common sense movement which answered Hume's scepticism by working out what 'common sense' tells us by self-evidence and necessary reasoning. However, he never provided an all-inclusive system of thought and the failure of his attack on Hume meant that his philosophy was eclipsed by that of Kant who did produce a comprehensive system of thought.[25] However, in many respects, Reid's more modest approach provided a better way forward than Kant's which led to an idealistic dead-end.

Reid's first book, *An Inquiry into the Mind on the Principles of Common Sense* (1764), deals with common sense in the original Aristotelian sense of *communis sensus* – the five senses of seeing, hearing, smelling, touching and tasting. Reid's answer to scepticism about our senses is to show how the five senses actually work in precise detail, thus laying the foundations for modern empirical psychology. These senses form the basis of our common sense view of the world which also gives rise to fundamental principles determined by our nature:

> If there are certain principles, as I think there are, which the constitution of our nature leads us to believe, and which we are under necessity to take for granted in the common concerns of life, without being able to give a reason for them – these are what we call the principles of common sense; and what is manifestly contrary to them, is what we call absurd.[26]

But it is arguable that these common sense principles take too much for granted and kill off metaphysical speculation in which we should take *nothing* for granted. In his later book, *Essays on the Intellectual Powers of Man* (1785), Reid gives us a long list of principles, the first of which is as follows: 'I shall take for granted, that I THINK, that I REMEMBER, that I REASON, and, in general, that I really perform all those operations of mind of which I am conscious.'[27] Reid argues that this principle is 'self-evident' and that therefore it is 'absurd' and against common sense to deny it. But this invites us to give up thinking altogether if we are to be as commonsensical as that. To this day, it is a puzzle just what consciousness is. We get nowhere if we take it for granted that consciousness consists only in being aware of our thinking, reasoning, remembering and performing operations of the mind. A lot more is involved in doing these things, but just what, is the big question. However, the common sense view is useful and persuasive in drawing attention to the immediacy of our experiences which do not involve reasoning about things. Our habits allow us to react automatically to everyday situations and this aspect of Reid's philosophy was later taken up by the pragmatist philosophers.

Perhaps Reid's philosophy is strongest in its comprehensive view of perception which attempts to incorporate the empiricist and rationalist views of perception:

> If we attend to that act of our mind which we call the perception of an external object of sense, we shall find in it these three things:-
> *First*, Some conception or notion of the object perceived; *Secondly*, A

strong and irresistible conviction and belief of its present existence; and, *Thirdly*, That this conviction and belief are immediate, and not the effect of reasoning.[28]

Here Reid includes acts of conception in the perceptual process, unlike the empiricists who thought of perception as being an immediate experience of percepts, images and thoughts. Reid was the first to confine the word 'perception' to the organs of sense. Previously, philosophers such as Locke and Hume referred to 'perceiving' thoughts and images. Reid also clarified the distinction between sensation and perception in a definitive way that is still with us today: '*I feel a pain; I see a tree*: the first denoteth a sensation, the last a perception.' Though the same grammar is used, the objects referred to are quite different. A pain doesn't exist apart from the feeling which accompanies it. It has no object and means nothing more than 'being pained'.[29] But perception is quite different:

> Perception, as we here understand it, hath always an object distinct from the act by which it is perceived; an object which may exist whether it be perceived or not. I perceive a tree that grows before my window; there is here an object which is perceived, and an act of the mind by which it is perceived; and these two are not only distinguishable, but they are extremely unlike in their natures. The object is made up of a trunk, branches, and leaves; but the act of the mind, by which it is perceived, hath neither trunk, branches, nor leaves. I am conscious of this act of mind, and I can reflect upon it; but it is too simple to admit of an analysis, and I cannot find proper words to describe it.[30]

Perception can therefore be seen as an interaction between our mental acts and the input from our sensory organs. Our perception of objects is constantly reinforced and corrected by this interaction. This interactive view of perception is better developed than Kant's rationalist account of perception that undervalues its role, so that Reid is superior to Kant at least in that respect.[31]

Immanuel Kant (1724–1804)

Even today, Kant is regarded by many people as being the greatest philosopher of all time. Certainly he is one of the most influential thinkers of all time. Kant's series of 'critiques' laid the foundations for the critical kind of society in which we now live. His first 'critique' is the *Critique of Pure Reason* (1787) which counters Hume's scepticism about our reasoning powers by working out the limits of these powers. Kant reacted to that scepticism by saying that it was 'scandal' to philosophy that we cannot account for the existence of external objects.[32] He believed that his 'architectonic' philosophy gave the ultimate answer to such doubts. It involved establishing the conditions which make our experience possible. He argued that pure reason by itself leads us astray by the antinomies and para-doxes to which it gives rise. The *Critique* is divided into two parts: the Analytic in which he lays down the basis of our reasoning powers and the Dialectic in which he shows the limits to pure reason.

The analytic/synthetic distinction

Kant begins by making an important distinction between the analytic and syn-thetic. An analytic proposition is true by definition – all bachelors are unmar-ried, whereas a synthetic proposition is derived from outwith the definition – all bachelors are looking for a good time. A big question for Kant is whether or not there can be synthetic *a priori* propositions. In other words, how can I get to know the world only by thinking about it, or how is rocket science so precise and reliable? Empiricism implies that only analytic *a priori* propositions can give us access to the world. But Kant thought that mathematics gives us synthetic and not analytic truths. Twentieth-century logicians such as Bertrand Russell disa-greed and argued that mathematics is analytical and therefore is founded on logic. This problem is still puzzling philosophers today.

Other unresolved problems raised by Kant in the *Critique of Pure Reason* include the paralogisms and antinomies of pure reason which show us the limits of our reasoning powers since they lead to absurdities. The paralogisms are fal-lacious syllogisms which concern such matters as whether the soul or thinking 'I' is a substance or identifiable thing. The antinomies are irresolvable illusions of which much can be said for both sides and no ultimate conclusions are pos-sible. These include whether or not the world has or has not a beginning in time, whether or not substances are made up of simple parts, or whether or not everything is caused and there is no possibility of freedom.

It is necessary to understand the technical terms that Kant uses. When these are understood then what he is saying is quite intelligible:

> In the analytical part of the Transcendental Logic we have shown that pure categories, and among them that of substance, have in themselves no objective meaning, save in so far as they rest upon an intuition [perception], and are applied to the manifold of this intuition, as functions of synthetic unity.[33]

Kant is saying here that our abstract concepts, such as substance, have no meaning in practice unless they are linked to objects of perception which are being perceived as a whole – a synthetic unity. In other words, 'Thoughts without content are empty, intuitions [perceptions] without concepts are blind.'[34]

Transcendental idealism

Kant is a 'rationalist' in that he thought that the conditions for empirical expe-rience are not discovered in experience but are reasoned out by us. We impose these conditions on our experience of reality. He called his idealism 'transcendental' because the conditions he was looking for *transcend* any experience. The transcending ego constructs knowledge by imposing universal concepts called categories on sense impressions. Objects are given to us within the intuitions of space and time, and they are conditioned by the categories (or 'concepts of the understanding') such as unity, plurality and causality. The resulting objects transcend experience in the way that trees are more than just a sum of their leaves, branches and trunk.

Transcendental idealism contrasts with what Kant called the 'sceptical idealism' of Descartes, who claimed that the existence of matter can be doubted, and with the 'dogmatic idealism'[35] of Berkeley, who denied the existence of matter altogether. Kant believed that ideas, the raw matter of knowledge, must refer to realities existing independently of the human mind. But these realities are things-in-themselves (*noumena*) which must remain forever unknown. Human knowledge cannot reach them because knowledge can only arise by synthesising the ideas of sense into the objects that we perceive or think about it (*phenomena*). Transcendentalism idealism means that we don't have direct contact with 'things in themselves' but only with representations of things. The thing in itself thus stands for an unrealisable ideal of context-free knowledge. This view ensured that his successors became idealists as they all strove to make more or less of the thing of itself than Kant dictated.

Against the run of his own arguments, Kant claimed to be both a transcendental idealist and an empirical realist. Both involve objectifying the world to make sense of it by the use of the intuitions of time and space and the concepts of the understanding to interact with the world. But the first involves a subjective point of view and the second an objective point of view. Instead of acknowledging the inevitable dualistic interaction implied by this distinction, Kant's idealism tended to predominate over his empiricist pretensions:

> The transcendental idealist, on the other hand, may be an empirical realist or, as he is called, a *dualist*; that is, he may admit the existence of matter without going outside his moral self-consciousness, or assuming anything more than the certainty of his representations, that is, the *cogito, ergo sum*. For he considers this matter and even its inner possibility to be appearance merely; and appearance, if separated from our sensibility, is nothing . . . . From the start, we have declared ourselves in favour of this transcendental idealism.[36]

Here Kant explicitly acknowledges the dualism at the heart of his philosophy but he fails to develop it because he favours one side, namely, transcendental idealism. If he were a consistent dualist he would say that we have direct access to things in themselves because of how we interact with our sensations and with the objects of perception, as was suggested by Reid. Because he did not specify what things in themselves really are, the idealist philosophers subsequently developed their own views in no uncertain terms, as we shall see.

The categorical imperative

Perhaps the most readable of Kant's books is the *Groundwork of the Metaphysics of Morals* (1785) which states his ethical views more straightforwardly than in his *Critique of Practical Reason* (1788). He regards us as being governed by a moral law which we freely use to regulate and make sense of our behaviour. This law is based on the categorical imperative which he distinguished from the hypothetical imperative which is more 'iffy':

> All imperatives command either *hypothetically* or *categorically*. Hypothetical imperatives declare a possible action to be practically necessary as a means to the attainment of something else that one wills (or that one may will). A categorical imperative would be one which represented an action as objectively necessary in itself apart from its relation to a further end.[37]
>
> When I conceive a hypothetical imperative in general, I do not know beforehand what it will contain – until its condition is given. But if I conceive a categorical imperative, I know at once what it contains. For since besides the law this imperative contains only the necessity that our maxim should conform to this law, while the law, as we have seen, contains no condition to limit it, there remains nothing over to which the maxim has to conform except the universality of a law as such; and it is this conformity alone that the imperative properly asserts to be necessary.
>
> There is therefore only a single categorical imperative and it is this: '*Act only on that maxim through which your will can at the same time will that it should become a universal law.*'[38]

The categorical imperative says that we must do only what we believe that everyone else should do in the same circumstances. It is a formal expression of the Golden Rule: 'Do to others what you would have them do to you.' Kant linked it with the need to do one's duty in all circumstances. This had a profound effect on the Victorian mentality which was often obsessed with doing its duty for duty's sake and not for any other reason. The notion of a moral law is incompatible with our current toleration of differences, which cannot be universally applied. If someone regards other people's sexual behaviour as being morally reprehensible then they should regard their view as a universal law and make vociferous objections to that form of behaviour. But we are not allowed to voice such objections nowadays. The universal law is one of universal toleration which itself is contradictory and unenforceable. It means that being intolerant of our behaviour is intolerable when people object to our intolerance of objectionable behaviour.

//

The French Enlightenment

The French Enlightenment followed the Scottish and English Enlightenments but differed from these in some important respects. Voltaire reputedly wrote: 'We look to Scotland for all our ideas on civilisation.' *(Nous nous tournons vers l'Écosse pour trouver toutes nos idées sur la civilisation.)* Unfortunately, French Revolutionaries such as Robespierre paid more attention to Rousseau than to Hume, Smith and Reid in implementing their revolution. Jean-Jacques Rousseau (1712–1778) argued in *The Social Contract* (1762) that our freedom must be 'alienated' to the community as a whole. This formula, namely, 'Each of us puts his person and all his power in common under the supreme direction of the general will' (ch. VI, para. 15) has been cheerfully used ever since by every tyrant and authoritarian regime to subjugate people. It is regrettable that postmodern philosophers focus on this aspect of the Enlightenment rather than on the achievements of the Enlightenment in general.

Simon Blackburn puts it this way:

> The West, it is sadly said, has lost confidence in the Enlightenment. It is quite common to see intellectuals state as a fact that the Enlightenment project has been tried and failed. This is a lie. There never was one single Enlightenment project, and of the Enlightenment projects that there were, many have succeeded beyond the wildest hopes of their proponents. The Enlightenment provided the matrix I have talked of, in which scientific enterprises could flourish. Now, our understanding of the world is better because of physical science. Our understanding of ourselves is better because of biological science. We live longer, and we feed ourselves better, and 'we' here includes not only people in first world countries, but countless people in the third world. We look after the environment better, and in time we will manage our own numbers better. Outside the theocracies of the east more people have more freedoms and enjoy more education, more opportunities and may even have more rights than ever before. We owe this progress entirely to the culture forged, in the west, by Bacon and Locke, Hume and Voltaire, Newton and Darwin. Humanism is the belief that humanity need not be ashamed of itself, and these are its great examples. They show us that we need not regard knowledge as impious, or ignorance as desirable, and we need not see blind faith as anything other than blind.[39]

Notes

1. David Hume (1777 edn), *An Enquiry Concerning Human Understanding*, ed. P.H. Nidditch, Oxford: Clarendon Press, 1975, Sect. V, Part I, p. 40.
2. Immanuel Kant (1784), *Beantwortung der Frage: Was ist Aufklärung?* In *Sämtliche Werke*, Fünfte Band, IV, p. 135. The quotation is from Horace, *Epodes*, 1, 2, 40.
3. George Berkeley (1710), *A Treatise Concerning the Principles of Human Knowledge*, in *A Treatise*

Concerning the Principles of Human Knowledge and Three Dialogues Between Hylas and Philonous, London: Collins, 1972, Introduction, §13, p. 53.

4. Ibid. Part I, §3, p. 66.
5. Ibid. Part I, §6, pp. 67–8.
6. Ibid. Part I, §110–117, pp. 119–24.
7. George Berkeley (1713), *Three Dialogues Between Hylas and Philonous,* in *A Treatise Concerning the Principles of Human Knowledge and Three Dialogues Between Hylas and Philonous,* London: Collins, 1972, Third Dialogue p. 236.
8. 'Journal of the Easy Club' (1712–1715), in *Works of Allan Ramsay,* ed. A. Kinghorn and A. Law, Vol. 5, Edinburgh: W. Blackwood, 1972, p. 31. The journal is usually attributed to John Fergus (born 1689), who was the secretary of the Easy Club, a merchant, and a tax collector for Edinburgh council.
9. Anonymous (1720), *An Account of the Fair Intellectual-Club in Edinburgh*: In a Letter to a Honourable Member of an Athenian Society there, By a young Lady, the Secretary of the Club, Edinburgh: Printed by J. M'Euen & Co., 1720, p. [i].
10. John Ramsay of Ochtertyre (1888), *Scotland and Scotsmen in the 18th Century,* ed. A. Allardyce, Edinburgh: W. Blackwood & Sons, 1888, Vol. I, pp. 195–6.
11. For more on the influences leading to the Scottish Enlightenment see Alistair J. Sinclair (1998a), 'The Emergence of Philosophical Inquiry in Eighteenth Century Scotland', unpublished PhD thesis 1998, Glasgow University Library, Thesis no. 11088.
12. David Hume (1739), *A Treatise of Human Nature,* ed. P.H. Nidditch, Oxford: Clarendon Press, 1989, Book I, Part I, Section I, p. 3.
13. David Hume (1777 edn), *An Enquiry Concerning the Principles of Morals,* ed. L.A. Selby-Bigge, Oxford: Clarendon Press, 1975, Sect. XII, Part III, §132, p. 165.
14. David Hume (1739), *A Treatise of Human Nature,* Book I, Part IV, Section VI, p. 252.
15. Ibid., Book I, Part III, Section XV, p. 173.
16. Ibid., Book II, Part III, Section III, p. 415.
17. Adam Smith (1759), *The Theory of Moral Sentiments,* London: H.G. Bohn, 1853, Part III, ch I, para. 2, p. 161.
18. Ibid., Part III, ch I, pp. 162–5.
19. Ibid., Part IV, ch I, pp. 264–5.
20. Adam Smith (1776), *An Inquiry into the Nature and Causes of the Wealth of Nations,* London: Routledge, *c.*1900, Book IV, ch. II, p. 345.
21. Ibid., Book I, ch. I, p. 4.
22. Ibid., Book I, ch. VIII, p. 63.
23. Ibid., Book I, ch. I, p. 8.
24. Thomas Reid (1764), *An Inquiry into the Mind on the Principles of Common Sense,* in *The Works of Thomas Reid,* ed. W. Hamilton, Edinburgh: J. Thin, 1895, ch. IV, sect. XX, p. 182b. 30. *Ibid.* p. 183b.
25. Cf. Alistair J. Sinclair (1995), 'The Failure of Thomas Reid's Attack on David Hume', *British Journal for the History of Philosophy,* Vol. 3, No. 2, pp. 389–98.
26. Thomas Reid (1764), *An Inquiry into the Mind on the Principles of Common Sense,* in *The Works of Thomas Reid,* ed. Hamilton, ch. II, sect. VI, p. 108b.
27. Thomas Reid (1785), *Essays on the Intellectual Powers of Man,* in *The Works of Thomas Reid,* ed. Hamilton, Essay I, ch. II, p. 231.
28. Ibid., Essay II, ch. V, p. 258a.
29. Thomas Reid (1764), *An Inquiry into the Mind on the Principles of Common Sense,* in *The Works of Thomas Reid,* ed. Hamilton, ch. IV, sect. XX, p. 182b.
30. Ibid. p. 183a.
31. For more on the Reid's theory of perception, see Alistair J. Sinclair (1993), 'Thomas Reid and the Perceptual Foundations of Knowledge', unpublished MPhil. thesis, University of Strathclyde Library, Thesis No. T 7562.
32. Immanuel Kant (1787), *A Critique of Pure Reason,* trans. N. Kemp Smith, London: Macmillan, 1964, Preface to 2nd edn, B xl fn, p. 34.
33. Ibid., A348/9, p. 333. There is a scene in the feature film, *Superman III,* where Pamela Stevenson is shown reading the *Critique of Pure Reason.* What she says indicates that she is reading this passage in the book.
34. Ibid., A51/B75, p. 93.
35. Ibid., A377, p. 350.
36. Ibid., A370, p. 346.

37. Immanuel Kant (1785), *The Moral Law* (*Groundwork of the Metaphysics of Morals*), trans. H.J. Paton, London: Hutchinson, 1972, p. 67.
38. Ibid., p. 84.
39. Simon Blackburn (2001), *Does Relativism Matter?* Voltaire Lecture for the British Humanist Association at King's College London, last para. Available in full at www.humanism.org.uk, and published in part in *The New Humanist*, Spring, 2002, pp. 14–15.

1.6 Nineteenth-Century Philosophy

Speculative philosophy, which to the superficial appears a thing so remote from the business of life and the outward interests of men, is in reality the thing on earth which influences them, and in the long run overbears every other influence save those which it must itself obey.

John Stuart Mill, 'Bentham' (1838)[1]

The nineteenth century heralded an age of idealism which fed on a reaction against the sterile, sceptical extremes of eighteenth-century empiricist philosophy. This idealism had practical down-to-earth origins in the hands of Fichte, but it later went towards its own extremes, especially in Hegel's philosophy. Idealist philosophy was led astray by a fruitless obsession with the Absolute which was ultimately a pantheistic quest for God-in-everything. Such a rationalisation could please neither theologians nor secularists and was doomed to failure. It failed philosophically because the idealists used the notion of the Absolute to answer the question: what is the relationship of mind to matter, mental to physical, or subject to object? Their answer took them increasingly into an absolutist stratosphere without any practical way of bringing us back down. This is the story of what went wrong and the resultant empiricist backlash which gave us analytical philosophy in the twentieth century and latterly postmodernism.

The German Idealists

Johann Gottlieb Fichte (1762–1814)

Fichte established German idealism as a distinct movement after he endured a long period without recognition. Without his efforts, Hegel's notoriously obscure philosophy would not have come to the fore as easily as it did. Hegel had the advantage of Fichte's reputation to build on and this enabled him to take idealism to its logical conclusion. Fichte also established German nationalism in 1807 with his Speeches to the German Nation (*Reden an die Deutsche Nation*). He roused the Germans to appreciate their own culture and oppose Napoleon's imposition of French culture on them.

In place of Kant's 'thing-in-itself', Fichte thought in terms of a *self-in-itself*. 'The thing-in-itself is a pure invention that has no reality whatsoever.'² The self was for him the basis of philosophy. In his *Science of Knowledge* (1802), Fichte distinguishes the self and not-self in a very dualistic fashion. The self is constantly differentiating itself from not-self by means of the moral law within that impels us to make the best of ourselves. But he argues that 'the self posits itself absolutely' and 'the self exists solely and absolutely through its positing of itself'.³ Thus, the absolute self becomes more important than the implied dualistic interaction between self and not-self. In this way, the Absolute was gradually isolated and came to dominate the German idealists' thinking.

Fichte saw human self-consciousness as the primary metaphysical fact through the analysis of which the philosopher finds his way to the cosmic totality that is 'absolute self' But this absolute self is not passive but is 'absolute activity and nothing other than activity'.⁴ Just as the moral will is the chief characteristic of the self, so it is also the activating principle of the world. He offered a new definition of philosophising to make it central in dignity in the intellectual world. The sole task of philosophy is 'the clarification of consciousness'. And the highest degree of self-consciousness is achieved by the philosopher because he alone recognises 'Mind' or 'Spirit' (*Geist*) as the central principle of reality. Unlike Hegel, Fichte always favoured action and he regarded reflection as justified only when it leads to worthwhile action:

> Not merely TO KNOW, but according to your knowledge TO DO, is your vocation . . . . Not for idle contemplation of yourself, not for brooding over devout sensations; – no, for action are you here; your action, and your action alone, determines your worth.⁵

As far as his successors were concerned, Fichte wasn't consistent enough in working out his idealist philosophy. Schelling and, more importantly, Hegel went beyond his views to work out a purer and more self-consistent idealism based on the Absolute.

Friedrich Wilhelm Joseph von Schelling (1775–1854)

Schelling was younger than Hegel who was a late developer and was influenced by Schelling rather than vice versa. Schelling revered Fichte as his philosophical model, until he realised that Fichte had not taken enough notice of nature in his philosophical system. Fichte always viewed nature as an object in subordination to man. Schelling, in contrast, wanted to show that Nature, seen in itself, develops towards Mind (*Geist*). He was much influenced by Spinoza's 'God or Nature' view. He argued that the scientific investigation of Nature makes us part of the natural order. But Nature is external to us and the opposite of the Mind which is within us. Mind should coincide with Nature rather than being alienated from it:

For what we want is not that Nature should coincide with the laws of our mind *by chance* (as if through some third intermediary), but that *she herself*, necessarily and originally, should not only *express* but *even realise*, the laws of our mind, and that she is called Nature only in so far as she does so. Nature is to be visible Mind, and Mind invisible Nature. Here then, in the absolute identity of Mind *in us* and Nature *outside us*, the problem of the possibility of a Nature external to us must be resolved.[6]

This seems to imply a dualistic interaction between Mind and Nature to maintain this 'absolute identity'. But Schelling aims for an absolutist monism. We become alienated from nature and practical action through self-conscious reflection. When reflection is made an end in itself, it becomes 'a spiritual sickness'.[7] Our subjective thinking becomes divorced from objectivity. However, philosophy, as 'a natural history of our minds',[8] can use reflection as a means to identify us absolutely with Nature. It works towards its own destruction by ending the separation between man and the world, and between subjectivity and objectivity. This means using such abstract notions as Mind, Nature, Idea and Absolute to reconcile the dualistic divide between subject and object. In so doing, he takes us further into idealism and away from practical application.

Schelling's philosophy of nature is his primary philosophical achievement and it made him well known in the circles of the Romantic poets of the early nineteenth century. Coleridge, in particular, was very much influenced by Schelling and he included passages from Schelling's work in his *Biographia Literaria* (1817).[9]

In his *System of Transcendental Idealism* (1800), Schelling attempted to unite his concept of Nature with Fichte's philosophy, which had taken the self as the point of departure. He argues that self-realisation requires concrete action in the world and this takes place in an organised state which becomes 'a second and higher Nature'. Whereas 'visible Nature' is governed mechanically by cause and effect, 'second Nature' allows freedom under the rule of law.[10] He saw the need for a federation of all the states which would eliminate conflict between states. Such a world organisation would result from historical progress which requires an ever greater understanding of the Absolute. Thus, everything comes from the Absolute which ultimately unifies subject and object and makes human consciousness redundant. Today it seems that the internet might eventually transcend human consciousness but, unlike the Absolute, it is entirely manmade and lacking in divinity. Fichte could not agree with Schelling's view of the Absolute as an agent of historical progress.

Georg Wilhelm Friedrich Hegel (1770–1831)

Hegel took Schelling's philosophy and developed it into a comprehensive system which was even more rigorously tied to the Absolute. He avoided Berkeley's idealistic extremes by acknowledging that reality is outside us. By thinking about reality, we get it inside our heads, but we have to think rigorously and logically to get it right. Logical thinking involves a dualistic opposition between a stated thesis and an antithesis which arises when contradictions in the thesis are made explicit. This opposition is resolved in a synthesis which then breaks down into a further thesis and antithesis. However, Hegel is prevented from developing a full-blown dualism because, like Schelling, his philosophy revolves round the Absolute into which everything is subsumed. He thinks of it as a monistic notion by which we grasp everything as a unified whole that is free of logical contradiction. However, it develops over time by means of the dialectic opposition between thesis and antithesis. We experience it as becoming rather than being since it actually exists only as an end:

> Of the Absolute it must be said that it is essentially a *result*, that only in the *end* is it what it truly is; and that precisely in this consists its nature, namely, to be actual, subject, the spontaneous becoming of itself.[11]

The Absolute amounts to the whole Truth which 'is the process of its own becoming, the circle that presupposes its end as its goal, having its end also as its beginning; and only by being worked out to its end, is it actual'.[12] Reality is therefore only graspable as a whole at the end of a dialectic process never completed by finite beings such as ourselves. Hegel takes a particularly historical view of this process. He argues that the philosopher's vocation is to approach the Absolute through consciousness and to recognise it as Mind (*Geist*) 'realising itself' in all of the manifold facets of human life. For struggle is the essence of spiritual existence, and self-enlargement is its goal. The various branches of intellect and culture become stages in the historical unfolding of the World-Mind. What begins in Hegel as a metaphysics of the Absolute ends by becoming a total philosophy of human culture.

Hegel believed that dogmatism is avoided by constantly thinking about everything in terms of abstractions such as the Absolute, Mind, Reason, Consciousness, Truth, Culture and Religion. Dogmatism involves having fixed and immutable ideas about things.[13] He was aiming for a science of the mind that accounts for our place in history. Such an idealism takes us in the wrong direction towards ever-increasing abstraction, and an obsession with Platonic ideas which are given a life of their own. Instead of following Hegel by unifying everything around one thing such as the Absolute or God, we can go on the other direction and, beginning with the origin of matter, we can show how human beings have arrived where they are by means of dualistic interaction with their environment. We may then arrive at a realistic view of our place in the universe instead of an idealistic one.

The influence of Hegelian idealism in Europe during the late nineteenth and early twentieth century explains the conformity and uniformity of the times.

Everyone was expected to have high ideals and defer to the authority of the State. In his *Philosophy of Right* (1821), Hegel not only idealises the State but positively deifies it:

> The State is the march of God through the world, its ground is the power of reason realising itself as will. The idea of the State should not denote any particular State, or particular institution; one must rather consider the Idea only, this actual God, by itself.[14]

Following Rousseau, Hegel argued that freedom is only obtainable within the state or wider community – a view rigorously applied by the Nazis in the twentieth century. The Hitlerian mantra *ein Volk, ein Reich, ein Führer* (one people, one nation, one leader) vividly expresses their state idealism, which effectively reduced an enlightened nation to a mindless mob in thrall to a God-like Absolute Leader to be obeyed without question.

Hegel's influence on Continental philosophy has continued up to the present day. His obscure, terminology-laden style of writing is still evident in postmodern philosophers such as Levinas and Habermas. Many of his terms are used in existentialist philosophy which is in many respects a development of Hegelian philosophy. Terms such as 'being-for-itself' and the 'other' are much used in Continental philosophy and feature in the following passage which exemplifies the obscurity of Hegel's writings:

> Self-consciousness is, to begin with, simple being-for-self, self-equal through the exclusion from itself of everything else. For it, its essence and absolute object is 'I'; and in this immediacy, or in this [mere] being, of its being-for-self, it is an *individual*. What is 'other' for it, is an unessential, negatively characterised object. But the 'other' is also a self-consciousness; one individual is confronted by another individual. Appearing thus immediately on the scene, they are for one another like ordinary objects, independent shapes, individuals submerged in the being [or immediacy] of *Life* – for the object in its immediacy is here determined as Life.[15]

Hegel is here referring to one individual person confronting another person. At first they are conscious of themselves alone and see the 'other' person as a physical object and as part of 'life'. This is the beginning of his well-known 'master–slave' argument. We are allegedly inclined to enslave one another unless we aspire to the reasonableness of the Absolute which enables us to make sense of other people being different from us. Cloaking such arguments in a tangled web of abstractions gives them the appearance of profundity and cleverness but it is not science as we now know it.

Later German Philosophers

Arthur Schopenhauer (1788–1860)

Schopenhauer is one of the bleakest and most pessimistic of philosophers. His influence has been overwhelmingly pernicious, yet he is still studied today because of the postmodern fashion for anti-Enlightenment thinkers who disparage the human race instead of appreciating it. Schopenhauer's principal philosophical work is *The World as Will and Representation* (1859). He begins this book with a relatively commonsensical account of perception. Indeed, in the second volume, he acknowledges his debt to Thomas Reid in formulating his views on perception.[16] However, he overlooks the directness of perception as described by Reid and adheres to the Kantian view that our perceptions only represent things and don't give us access to 'things-in-themselves'.

Schopenhauer's view was that we arrive at our concepts of things by acts of will, that is to say, by thinking about them and acting in relation to them. The will is the spirit behind everything so that it is 'the thing in itself'. However, this will is not a liberating but an imprisoning thing. We are enslaved by our wills because we are always desiring, striving, asserting ourselves and conflicting with other people. By progressive denials of the will, we relieve ourselves of worldly suffering and gravitate towards 'empty nothingness'.[17] Thus Schopenhauer advocates an eastern asceticism as the be-all and end-all of human existence. He arrives at this anti-social and unhumanistic position in response to the alleged suffering of the world which he argues is due to our wilfulness. This view is obviously attractive to present-day sceptics and pessimists who see no future for the human race on this planet which we are currently destroying irreparably. But the fact is that our knowledge of this situation means that we can and must do something about it, even if it makes no difference in the end. Logically, Schopenhauer's views imply that mass suicide is the best way to get rid of suffering and to deny the will absolutely. However, he contrives some strained arguments to avoid this conclusion, for example, by saying that denying the will-to-live does not mean denying life.[18] In short, Schopenhauer's is a sad loser's philosophy which was directly responsible for the suicides of many young men in its heyday during the late nineteenth century. The bizarre lifestyles of his most famous disciples, Nietzsche and Wittgenstein, confirm this. The fact that Adolf Hitler claimed to be a disciple of Schopenhauer explains a lot about his imbecility.[19]

In Schopenhauer's view, we can escape enslavement by the will through two ways: either that of aesthetic contemplation or of asceticism. But both these ways smack of the vacuity of nirvana:

> Aesthetic pleasure in the beautiful consists, to a large extent, in the fact that, when we enter the state of pure contemplation, we are raised for the moment above all willing, above all desires and cares; we are, so to speak, rid of ourselves. We are no longer the

individual that knows in the interest of its constant willing, the correlative of the particular thing to which objects become motives, but the eternal subject of knowing purified of the will, the correlative of the Idea. And we know that these moments, when, delivered from the fierce pressure of the will, we emerge, as it were, from the heavy atmosphere of the earth, are the most blissful that we experience. From this we can infer how blessed must be the life of a man whose will is silenced not for a few moments, as in the enjoyment of the beautiful, but forever, indeed completely extinguished, except for the last glimmering spark that maintains the body and is extinguished with it.[20]

All in all, Schopenhauer's philosophy exemplifies the harm that negative ideas can do when they are taken seriously. His use of eastern thinking was a mistake as western thinking was bound to triumph over it since the former was clearly going nowhere and achieving nothing, as the current widespread adoption of western values shows.

Friedrich Wilhelm Nietzsche (1844–1900)

Like Schopenhauer, Nietzsche is undeservedly fashionable today. At best, he is an aphoristic poet-philosopher whose most important work is *Thus Spake Zarathustra* (1885). It is an enthralling and highly readable work which belongs to prophetic literature rather than to philosophy. Otherwise, his thinking was distorted and obsessed with suffering, as his other writings show. This view is endorsed by Michael Tanner in his authoritative account: 'He was possessed by a vision of the world as a place of such horror that any attempt to give meaning to it in moral terms is simply impossible.'[21] Nevertheless, there is much of interest to be gleaned from his writings as long as they treated as insightful rather than truthful. For instance, his insights into morality and the human condition challenge us to show what's wrong with them, if we believe them to be so. Such books as *Beyond Good and Evil* (1886) and *On the Genealogy of Morals* (1887) strongly influenced postmodern philosophers such as Derrida. However, Nietzsche was reacting against the austere Germanic morality of the late nineteenth century. Perhaps he usefully guides those overburdened with morality, but his ramblings surely offer little concrete guidance to those with no previous conception of it.

Nietzsche never came to terms with the complexities of the modern world, for two reasons in particular. Firstly, as a philosopher, he was little more than a disciple of Schopenhauer, which meant that he was forever running away from the world in a vain search for aesthetic contemplation. Secondly, he trained as a classical philologist and was steeped in Greek literature. His ideal society was therefore Classical Greece before Socrates whose disciples, in his view, rationalised it out of existence. His poor understanding of the scientific, technological and economic achievements of the modern world meant that he harked back to ancient Greece as a golden age. Thus, in his unsuccessful first book, *The Birth of Tragedy* (1872), he favours the Dionysian excesses of Greek culture as opposed to the Apollonian rationalism which prevailed because of philosophers such as Plato and Aristotle.

He exceeded Schopenhauer's view of the Will by emphasising the Will to Power. But he really means the power of the artist to exert his will in seeking artistic self-expression. He had no interest in promoting political or other forms of power. His 'superman' was thus an artistic hero and was not superior either racially or in evolutionary terms. The Nazis distorted his writings in that regard.

If Nietzsche had understood contemporary society better, he might have recognised the liberal advances being achieved in Britain and America. He probably never read De Tocqueville's *Democracy in America* (1835). On the one hand, he rails against the slave morality of Christianity; on the other hand, he objects to J.S. Mill's 'offensive clarity' and 'the 'improvers' of mankind'.[22] He also failed to understand Darwin's theory of evolution. He says that Darwin 'forgot the mind' as the clever 'weak' often triumph over the strong.[23] He fails to understand that evolution does not perfect the species but enables them to adapt, often in spite of weakness. It applies only to animal species over countless millennia, and not to cultural change brought about by physically 'weak' human beings.

Nietzsche wrongly thought that when the authority of religion is overthrown, a nihilistic view is inevitable, namely, that the world is valueless, purposeless and amounts to nothing:

> The most extreme form of nihilism would be the view that *every* belief, every considering-something-true, is necessarily false because there simply is no *true world* . . . . To this extent, nihilism as the denial of a truthful world, of being, might be a *divine way of thinking.*[24]

Nietzsche failed to appreciate that truth is a process and not an end in itself. We are responsible for creating our own values and finding our own meaning in life. Religion is just one way of doing this and has become inadequate for our present purposes. Presumably, his theory of eternal recurrence prevented him from thinking of cultural change and improvement since, in his view, everything comes back to the same thing in the end.[25] In that case, we needn't bother about anything. There is no evidence for such a belief; it is merely an excuse for being and doing nothing.

Søren Kierkegaard (1813–1855)

Kierkegaard was a Danish rather than a German philosopher but he reacted against Hegelian idealism and developed the first existentialist philosophy by emphasising the 'angst' or 'anxiety' of life. He believed that awareness of one's own existence is most acute during periods of extreme inner tension when anxiety and dread of life become total and therefore metaphysical. Only in states of extreme emotional crisis when we face our possible or imminent annihilation do we finally grasp the significance of our existence. In our modern view, his disposition seems morbid and self-obsessive. However, his views perhaps explain the attraction of dangerous and life-threatening sports and activities since, in facing our dread of death, we intensify our experience of life.

Kierkegaard's ideas were intertwined with his own life as can be seen from an extract from his journal, concerning Regine, to whom he was engaged for a year or so:

> But if I had explained myself to her, I would have had to initiate her into terrible things, my relationship with my father, his melancholy, the eternal night brooding within me, my going astray, lusts, and excesses, which perhaps in God's eyes are not so glaring; for it was, after all, anxiety which made me go astray.[26]

Here we have the key to his book, *The Concept of Anxiety* (1844). Through anxiety, he falls from innocence into sin, and his Christian beliefs lead him from guilt to faith. In his view, anxiety precedes sin rather than following it. Religion usually provides some comfort and solace, but Kierkegaard's plight shows how excessive religiosity merely intensifies morbidity and self-absorption. Such extremism expresses itself either inwardly in morbid feelings of self-abnegation, as with Kierkegaard, or outwardly in nasty acts of destructive fanaticism.

Kierkegaard attacked Hegel's attempt to systematise the whole of existence, declaring that a system of existence cannot be constructed, since existence is incomplete and constantly developing. He drew attention to the logical error inherent in Hegel's attempt to introduce mobility into logic and so revealed the confusion arising from the mixing of categories. Hegel thought he had created an objective theory of knowledge but Kierkegaard argued that subjectivity is truth or, to quote his own definition, 'An objective uncertainty maintained in the most passionate spirit of dedication is truth, the highest truth for one existing.'[27] He goes on:

> When subjectivity, inwardness, is the truth, the truth becomes objectively a paradox; and the fact that the truth is objectively a paradox shows in its turn that subjectivity is the truth . . . The paradoxical character of the truth is its objective uncertainty; this uncertainty is an expression for the passionate inwardness, and this passion is precisely the truth.[28]

One may wonder how truth based on our passions can be regulated if not by objective correspondence to external realities. Kierkegaard's scepticism is of the wrong sort. We need to be sceptical and uncertain of our inner passions and impulses more than we are of our objective experiences of external reality. Otherwise we would be ruled entirely by our feelings rather than by our factual knowledge and by our judgement concerning what we ought or ought to do about our plight.

Karl Marx (1818–1883)

Marx turned Hegel on his head by making the 'Absolute' material instead of ideal; hence what his followers called 'dialectic materialism'. For him, materialism meant that the material world, perceptible to the senses, has an objective reality independent of mind. He didn't deny the reality of mental or spiritual processes but argued that ideas arise only from reflection on material conditions. He understood materialism as the opposite of idealism, by which he meant any theory that treats matter as dependent on mind, and capable of existing independently of mind.

Nevertheless, Marx's conception of dialectics owes much to Hegel, who saw change and development as the expression of the Absolute, which realises itself in nature and in human society. However, for Marx, change was inherent in the nature of the material world. He started from the materialist premise that all knowledge is derived from the senses. Against the mechanistic view that derives knowledge exclusively from given sense impressions, he stressed the dialectical development of human knowledge, which is socially acquired in the course of practical activity. Individuals can gain knowledge of objects only through their practical interaction with those objects. They must frame their ideas corresponding to their practice, and social practice alone provides the test of the correspondence of ideas with reality, that is, of truth. This theory of knowledge is opposed (1) to subjective idealism, according to which individuals can know only sensible appearances while things-in-themselves are elusive, and (2) to objective idealism, according to which individuals can know supersensible reality by pure intuition or thought, independent of sense.

Marx's economic views, famously expounded in the voluminous *Capital* (1867), were doomed to failure from the very first sentence of the book where he assumes that the production of 'commodities' is the source of all economic wealth.[29] The importance of services in contributing to wealth never occurred to him. He therefore thought that manual workers were more important than capitalists because commodities cannot be produced without them. He underestimated the importance of middlemen in relieving bottlenecks in the economy and contributing to efficiency and cost savings. In his view, 'commercial crises' result not, as we now know, from a failure to understand the complex workings of the economy, but 'because there is too much civilisation, too much means of subsistence, too much industry, too much commerce'.[30] Thus, communism has always interfered with capitalism's ability to heal itself and move on. Capitalism has constantly evolved into different forms in different countries in ways that

Marx could not have anticipated. As a social system, it is also capable of becoming more humane and rational as long as it is subjected to constant scrutiny and criticism in an open society.

Marx's social theories were flawed in that he was captivated by the Hegelian view that the individual is subordinate to the state. He thought that we can only be free by controlling society and ridding it of class divisions. This led to his famous saying: 'From each according to his ability, to each according to his needs'.[31] This implies that the state must know in advance our abilities and needs so that it can to tell us what to do about them. In other words, our freedom is to be thrust upon us, Rousseau-fashion, by authoritarian means. Instead, our freedom lies surely in our accomplishing what we aim to do, both individually and collectively. The social structure is then adjusted in accordance with these aims rather than being engineered by a predetermined utopian plan.

Marx also famously wrote: 'The philosophers have only *interpreted* the world in different ways; the point is to change it.'[32] On the contrary, the world has been changed constantly by the different interpretations that philosophers have put on it. For example, the effects of Hegel's and Mill's respective philosophies are obvious and widespread. Marx clearly wants to change the world without interpreting it. He prefers irrational revolution to measured rational change, with all the unnecessary chaos and misery that ensues from such an anarchic view.

Marx's political and economic views were also put into question by the fall of communist regimes in Eastern Europe from 1989 onwards. But there remains much of philosophical interest in his writings, for example, his attempt to convert idealism into a materialism. Indeed, many postmodern philosophers were influenced by Marx, if not themselves 'Marxists' (even though Marx reputedly said 'All I know is that I am not a Marxist'.[33])

Nineteenth-Century Empiricists

John Stuart Mill (1806–1873)

Mill had one of the most developed intellects of all time. His inborn talents were honed to an awesome perfection by a relentless educational programme imposed on him by his father from an early age. He famously resented being deprived of a boyhood and suffered a mental breakdown when adjusting to adulthood. Nevertheless, his spirit prevailed over such hardships and he produced a series of enduring works of philosophy. In particular, he changed the world by laying the foundations of liberal democracy with his *Essay on Liberty* (1859) and his *Representative Government* (1861). It is surely no coincidence that two years after Mill became a Member of Parliament in 1865, Disraeli passed his Reform Bill extending the vote to all male householders.

Mill's *System of Logic* (1843) is very well written and highly readable considering the difficulty of the subject matter. Its 'system' is not however very rigorous or consistent. He defines logic in at least half-a-dozen different ways, for example,: 'the Art of Reasoning', 'the theory of Argumentation' and 'the science of the operations of the understanding subservient to the estimation of evidence'.[34] The book is of interest today because he tries to show that mathematics is derived from our experience, and he emphasises the inductive side of logic as opposed to the deductive. His arguments have been severely criticised by logicians such as Frege. The passages in the book on freedom and determinism are also still relevant to the current debate on these topics.[35]

In his *Principles of Political Economy* (1848), Mill argues for a fairer distribution of wealth and aimed for the common welfare of the people. Remarkably, he advocates a 'stationary society' in which he believes, rather optimistically, we can get out of the rat-race of competitive society by no longer striving for wealth and never-ending economic growth.[36] This was obviously written before Darwin and his disciples argued us into being competitive animals forever striving to perpetuate our genes.

His essay 'On the Subjection of Woman' (1869) provides the philosophy that led to the suffragette movement and eventually to the feminist movement. He is quite forthright about the differences between men and women, for example: 'Do we not find that the things in which men most excel women are those which require most plodding and long hammering at a single thought, while women do best what must be done rapidly?'[37]

Mill's only failure lay in his utilitarian ethics which he was never able to work out satisfactorily. In inheriting the doctrine of utilitarianism from his dominant father, he was unable or unwilling to see beyond the principle of 'the greatest happiness of the greatest number' as being the best basis for a comprehensive ethical theory. This principle is flawed in implying that society exists only to make everyone happy. If that were so, we could induce universal felicity by issuing everyone with alcohol, drugs and cigarettes free and on demand. Even then, not everyone would be happy, as one person's happiness is another's hell. We are often unsure what makes us happy and we resent people making things easy for us by enforcing happiness. Mill recognises the strength of such arguments when he says such things as: 'It is better to be a human being dissatisfied than a pig satisfied; better to be Socrates dissatisfied than a fool satisfied.'[38] But the more he stresses the importance of doing our duty and not expecting to be happy all the time, the more he undermines the greatest happiness principle without putting something better in its place.

William James (1842–1910)

James was an American philosopher and the brother of the novelist, Henry James, and he trained as a doctor before making his name with the magisterial *Principles of Psychology* (1890); still considered by some to be an unsurpassed, general survey of psychology. But he is most renowned as an exponent of pragmatic philosophy which he outlines in his classic account *Pragmatism* (1907). This is the view that an idea, opinion, proposition or theory is true or right in so far as it can be successfully applied to the world. If two competing theories offer no immediate practical differences, then the best theory may be established by considering the effects or consequences of believing in one or the other. One theory will have more 'cash-value' if it leads to more successful living than the other theory:

> If there is any life that it is really better we should lead, and if there be any idea which, if believed in, would help us to lead that life, then it would be really *better for us* to believe in that idea, *unless, indeed, belief in it incidentally clashed with other greater vital benefits.*[39]

According to this view, the workability of our ideas and theories is shown by the satisfactory consequences of treating them as true. This makes truth a subjective matter which is to be decided by each of us for ourselves. It leads to modern 'relativism' in which we are to tolerate different beliefs which are true for someone else, and regardless of whether they are objectively true or fit into our culture.

James struggles valiantly against such dire consequences by developing a theory of truth which was not accepted by C.S. Peirce (1839–1914), the founder of pragmatism, who famously renamed his own philosophy 'pragmaticism' in response.[40] Peirce thought that pragmatism should be confined to clarifying meanings and need not enter thorny matters of truth. James overworks the workability of truth by attempting to explain all aspects of it using such terms as 'workable', 'practical', 'better', 'satisfactory' and 'instrumental'. He wrote *The Meaning of Truth* (1909) in response to fierce criticisms of his original account of truth but the more he strives to explain truth in such narrow terms, the more complex and unworkable his theory becomes, and it has never yet satisfied its critics.

As if pragmatism were not enough, James gives us 'cash-value' with two philosophies for the price of one, namely, pragmatism and 'radical empiricism' as he calls it. James begins his *Pragmatism* book by acknowledging the dualistic distinction between empiricism and rationalism. He clearly sees that they are opposing but unavoidable attitudes of mind. But he fails to conclude that we need both attitudes of mind to be balanced, truth-seeking persons. He might have developed pragmatism as a dualist philosophy but he decides in favour of empiricism and disparages 'rationalism' as being 'tender-minded' as opposed to 'tough-minded' empiricism.[41]

Whereas pragmatism has 'no doctrines save its method',[42] radical empiricism is a systematic philosophy that represents James's world view. Radical empiricism is not necessary to pragmatism as it can 'stand on its own feet. One may entirely reject it and still be a pragmatist.'[43] On the other hand, the pragmatist theory of truth can play a necessary role in helping radical empiricism to prevail.[44]

British Hegelian philosophy

During the nineteenth century, German idealism took over as the dominant philosophy in Britain. As already noted, Coleridge and the Romantic poets were much influenced by Schelliing. Ironically, the first of the British Hegelian philosophers was also the last of the Scottish common sense philosophers. This was James Ferrier (1808–1864). Because Thomas Reid and his immediate successor, Dugald Stewart, failed to work out common sense philosophy in a systematic and convincing way, the Scottish philosophers became increasingly interested in the German philosophers. This culminated in Ferrier's *Institutes of Metaphysics* (1854) which is a distinctly Hegelian work. He looked down on Reid's 'common' views: 'At home in the submarine abysses of popular opinion, Dr. Reid, in the higher regions of philosophy, was as helpless as a whale in a field of clover.'[50] He found in Hegel the clear doctrines that he failed to find in Reid.

Hegelian philosophy dominated British thinking during the last quarter of the nineteenth century when empirical philosophers such as Hume went out of fashion. Empiricism was more evident on the Continent in the work of men such as Ernst Mach (1838–1916), Franz Brentano (1838–1917), Henri Poincaré (1854–1912) and Henri Bergson (1859–1941). Prominent British Hegelian philosophers include T.H. Green (1836–1882), F.H. Bradley (1846–1903), Bernard Bosanquet (1848–1923), and John McTaggart (1866–1925). Bradley is still widely read for his *Appearance and Reality* (1897), and his ethical works. McTaggart is important for his theory of time which still vexes philosophers today. Both these philosophers influenced Moore and Russell who then reacted against them and turned British philosophy back to realism and empiricism. Ironically, the spirit of Thomas Reid has its vengeance on idealism through G.E. Moore, who used Reid's common sense views in his reaction against idealism.

His empiricism is 'radical' because it is a pluralism with a monistic basis, namely, the one thing that is true of the world is that it is pluralistic. Unlike Hume's empiricism which views the world as comprising unconnected experiences, radical empiricism views causation and other relationships between objects as being part of the universal pluralism of the world.[45] It deals with what our experiences are like in an ever-changing pluralistic universe. In effect, James is reacting against the monistic idealism of the Hegelians rather than incorporating it in his own thinking.[46] Radical empiricism has served to associate pragmatism with empiricism in opposition to rationalism. Thus, pragmatism, along with analytical philosophy, contributed to the divided thinking which led to the left–right political divisions of the twentieth century and ultimately to the extremes of communism and fascism.

The effect of pragmatism has also been to perpetuate absolute religious belief instead of making it provisional and contingent. Thus, James said: 'Believe that life *is* worth living, and your belief will help create the fact.'[47] But this assertion of belief can equally characterise a fundamentalist or extremist view. We are expected to believe absolutely without further thought on the matter. But if we think for ourselves, we need *reasons* for believing and this has always been the role of philosophy as compared with religion which too often obliges us to believe full stop. This toleration of absolute belief has ensured that pragmatism legitimises any belief by saying 'If that works for you, that's great!'[48]

Perhaps William James's most popular book is his *Varieties of Religious Experience* (1902), in which he fully and lucidly points out the horrors and extremes of religious belief as well as the benefits of 'healthy-minded' religious belief. He comes down in favour of religion but makes no attempt to offer a new religion for humankind. But perhaps his own views are summed up by Professor Leuba whom he quotes as saying:

> Not God, but life, more life, a larger, richer, more satisfying life, is the end of religion. The love of life at any and every level of development, is the religious impulse.[49]

Notes

1. John Stuart Mill (1838), 'Bentham', in *Utilitarianism and Other Essays*, Harmondsworth: Penguin, 1987, p. 132.
2. J.G. Fichte (1802), *Science of Knowledge*, trans. P. Heath and J. Lachs, Cambridge: Cambridge University Press, 1982, Introduction, p. 10.
3. Ibid., Part III, §5, p. 222.
4. Ibid., Part III, §5, p. 221.
5. J.G. Fichte (1800), *The Vocation of Man*, trans. W. Smith, Lasalle: Open Court, 1965, p. 94.
6. W.J. von Schelling (1797), *Ideas for a Philosophy of Nature, as Introduction to the Study of This Science*, trans. Errol E. Harris and Peter Heath, Cambridge: Cambridge University Press, 1988, pp. 41–2.
7. Ibid., p. 11.
8. Ibid., p. 30.
9. Samuel Taylor Coleridge (1817), *Biographia Literaria*, London: J.M. Dent, 1975, Chs.VIII–IX, pp. 75–87.
10. W.J. von Schelling (1800), *System of Transcendental Idealism*, trans. Peter Heath, Charlottesville: University Press of Virginia, 1978, Part Four, Section III, p. 195.
11. G.W.F. Hegel (1807), *Phenomenology of Spirit*, trans. A.V. Miller, Oxford: Oxford University Press, 1979, Preface, p11.
12. Ibid., p. 10.
13. Ibid., p. 23.
14. G.W.F. Hegel (1821), *Philosophy of Right*, trans. T.M. Knox, Oxford: Clarendon Press, 1942, §255, Add. 152, p. 279. See also §272, Add. 164, p. 285: 'Man must therefore venerate the State as a secular deity.'
15. G.W.F. Hegel (1807), *Phenomenology of Spirit*, ch. IV, A, §186, p. 113.
16. Arthur Schopenhauer (1859), *The World as Will and Representation*, New York: Dover, 1966, Vol. II, pp. 20–21.
17. Ibid. Vol. I, p. 409.
18. Ibid. Vol. I, pp. 398–9.
19. Cf. Adolf Hitler, *Hitler's Table Talk, 1941–1944*, trans. Norman Cameron and R.H. Stevens, London: Weidenfeld & Nicolson, 1953, 16 May 1944, §327, p. 720: 'I carried Schopenhauer's works with me throughout the whole of the First World War. From him I learned a great deal.'
20. Arthur Schopenhauer (1859), *The World as Will and Representation*, Vol. I, p. 390.
21. Michael Tanner (1994), *Nietzsche*, Oxford: Oxford University Press, Past Masters Series, 1994, p. 17. Now republished as 'A Very Short Introduction'.
22. Friedrich Nietzsche (1889), *Twilight of the Idols*, Harmondsworth: Penguin, 1968, 'The "Improvers" of Mankind', p. 55; also 'Expeditions of an Untimely Man' §1, p. 67.
23. Ibid., 'Expeditions of an Untimely Man', §14, pp. 76–7.

24. Friedrich Nietzsche (1901), *The Will to Power*, trans. W. Kaufmann, New York: Vintage Books, 1968, ¶ 15, pp. 14–15.
25. Cf. ibid. ¶ 55, pp. 35–6; ¶ 617, p. 330; ¶ 1053–67, pp. 543–50. See also Friederich Nietzsche, *Thus Spoke Zarathustra* (1885), trans. R.J. Hollindale, Harmondsworth: Penguin, 1967, Part Three, 'The Convalescent', pp. 237–8.
26. Søren Kierkegaard (1978), *Journals and Papers*, ed. and trans. H.V. Hong and E.H. Hong, Bloomington: Indiana University Press, 1978, Vol. 5, Part One, 1829–1848, ¶5664, May 17, 1843, p. 234.
27. Søren Kierkegaard (1846), *Concluding Unscientific Postscript*, trans. D.F. Swenson, Princeton: Princeton University Press, 1974, ch. II, p. 182.
28. Ibid., p. 183.
29. Karl Marx (1867), *Capital*, London: J.M. Dent, 1972, Book One, Part One, ch.1, p. 3.
30. Karl Marx (1848), *Manifesto of the Communist Party*, Moscow: Progress Publishers, 1973, ch. I, p. 50.
31. Karl Marx (1875), *Critique of the Gotha Programme*, as quoted in *Selected Writings in Sociology and Social Philosophy*, ed. T.B. Bottomore and M. Rubel, Harmondsworth: Penguin, 1973, Part Five, p. 263.
32. Karl Marx (1845), *Theses on Feuerbach*, as quoted in *Selected Writings in Sociology and Social Philosophy*, ed. T.B. Bottomore and M. Rubel, Part One, ch. 2, §XI, p. 84.
33. According to Friedrich Engels in a letter to C. Schmidt, 5 August 1890. Cf. Peter Singer (1980), *Marx*, Oxford: Oxford University Press, Past Masters Series, 1983, p. 38. Now republished as 'A Very Short Introduction'.
34. J.S. Mill (1843), *A System of Logic: Ratiocinative and Inductive*, London: Longman, 1970, Introduction, §2, p. 1; §3, p. 2; §7, p. 6 respectively.
35. Ibid., Book VI, Ch. II, pp. 547–8.
36. J.S. Mill (1848), *Principles of Political Economy* (Books IV and V), ed. Donald Winch, Harmondsworth: Penguin, 1970, Book IV, Ch. VI, §2, p. 113.
37. J.S. Mill (1869), 'The Subjection of Women' (in *Three Essays by J.S. Mill*), London: Oxford University Press, 1971, p. 505.
38. J.S. Mill (1863), *Utilitarianism*, London: Collins, 1964, ch. II, p. 260.
39. William James (1907), *Pragmatism*, Cambridge, Massachusetts: Harvard University Press, 1975, Lecture Two, p. 42.
40. Cf. C.S. Pierce (1905), 'The Essentials of Pragmatism', in *Philosophical Writings of Pierce*, New York: Dover, 1955, ch. 17, p. 255: 'The writer . . . begs to announce the birth of the word "pragmaticism", which is ugly enough to be safe from kidnapping'.
41. William James (1907), *Pragmatism*, Lecture One, p. 13.
42. Ibid., Lecture Two, [p. 27.] p. 32.
43. Ibid., Preface, p. 6.
44. William James (1909), *The Meaning of Truth*, Cambridge, Massachusetts: Harvard University Press, 1975, Preface, p. 6.
45. Cf., for example, William James (1912), *Essays in Radical Empiricism*, Lincoln: University of Nebraska Press, 1996, ch. II, pp. 42–3.
46. William James (1909), *A Pluralistic Universe*, Lincoln: University of Nebraska Press, 1996, Lecture II, p. 43.
47. William James (1897), *The Will to Believe*, New York: Dover, 1956, 'Is Life Worth Living?' p. 62, last paragraph.
48. Cf. Simon Blackburn (2001), *Being Good: A Short Introduction to Ethics*, Oxford: Oxford University Press, 2001, ch. 2, p. 26.
49. William James (1902), *The Varieties of Religious Experience*, London: Fontana, 1974, Conclusions, p. 483.
50. James Ferrier (1854), *Institutes of Metaphysics*, Edinburgh: W. Blackwood, 1854, Sect. II, Prop. IX, para 18, p. 495.

1.7 Twentieth-Century Philosophy

> Ever since men became capable of free speculation, their actions, in innumerable important respects, have depended upon their theories as to the world and human life, as to what is good and what is evil. This is as true in the present day as at any former time. To understand an age or a nation, we must understand its philosophy, and to understand its philosophy we must ourselves be in some degree philosophers.
>
> Bertrand Russell, *History of Western Philosophy* (1946)[1]

Philosophy in twentieth-century Britain began with the dominance of idealism which fuelled jingoism, imperialism and a fervent belief in 'God, King and Country' that contributed to the mindless slaughter of the 1914–18 war. The reaction against Victorian idealism led to the dominance of analytical philosophy. Thus, there was a swing from dogmatic rationalism to dogmatic empiricism. The failure of these extreme philosophies to make a lasting contribution to human understanding led to increasing scepticism about philosophy among professional philosophers. This culminated in Rorty's *Philosophy and the Mirror of Nature* (1979) which dogmatically argues that there never will be a 'foundation' on which to found our knowledge of things. Continental philosophy, meanwhile, followed its largely Hegelian path with phenomenology, existentialism, and latterly postmodernism which has attempted to marry analytical scepticism about philosophical problems with idealist obscurantism and Marxist dogmatism. A forcefully expressed philosophy is welcome as long as (1) it is engaging and productive and (2) its provisional and limited nature is freely acknowledged. Unfortunately, a passionate belief in the truth of one's conclusions is as common in philosophy as it is in both science and religion.

G.E. (George Edward) Moore (1873–1958)

Moore began the revolt against Hegelian idealism and laid the foundations of analytical philosophy with his 1899 paper called 'The Nature of Judgment'.[2] Russell later admitted that: 'Moore led the way, but I followed closely in his footsteps.'[3] Moore's paper emphasised analytical truth as against the relational truth sought by idealists. We find truth by analysing the content of our judgements instead of relating that content to the bigger picture. Thus, logical analysis becomes more important than the synthesis favoured by the idealists.

Moore is perhaps better known nowadays for his contribution to ethical theory with his *Principia Ethica* (1903). The last chapter of the book argues that we should avoid 'evil or ugly' things and appreciate 'beauty in Art and Nature'.[4] Such views motivated the aestheticism of the Bloomsbury Set which included Virginia Woolf and J.M. Keynes. More importantly, Moore contended that most ethical philosophers make a mistake that he called the 'Naturalistic Fallacy'.[5] This is the fallacy of defining the word 'good' by its natural qualities as if it were a material object. The business of ethics is to discover the qualities that make things good. For example, hedonists claim that the quality of *being pleasant* makes things good, while other theorists could claim that *complexity* is what makes things good. Moore has no quarrel with these contentions. He objects to the idea that the qualities making things good give us an analysis of the term 'good' and of the property 'goodness'. In his view, this is a serious confusion. A hedonist might be right to claim that something is good when it is pleasant. But this does not mean that we can define good in terms of pleasure. Following his study of Thomas Reid's views, Moore contended that goodness cannot be analysed in terms of any other property:

> Far too many philosophers have thought that when they named those other properties they were actually defining good; that these properties, in fact, were simply not 'other,' but absolutely and entirely the same with goodness.[6]

The only definition we can give of 'good' is an ostensive one; that is, we can only point to an action or a thing and say 'That is good.' Similarly, we cannot describe to a blind man exactly what yellow is. We can only show a sighted man a piece of yellow paper or a yellow scrap of cloth and say 'That is yellow.' Moore argued that when naturalistic fallacy arguments have been discarded, questions of goodness could only be settled by appeal to 'moral intuitions'. These are self-evident propositions which recommend themselves to moral reflection, but which are not susceptible to either direct proof or disproof.[7] As a result of his view, he has often been considered to be an ethical intuitionist.

Moore was much influenced by Thomas Reid's common sense views which he modified for his own purposes. In his essay 'A Defence of Common Sense' (1925) he argued, against idealism and scepticism towards the external world, that no reasons can be given that are more plausible than our common sense claims about our knowledge of the world. He famously put the point dramatically in his 'Proof of an External World' (1939). He gives a common sense argument against scepticism by raising his right hand and saying 'Here is one hand' and then raising his left and saying 'And here is another.'[8] He concluded that there are at least two external objects in the world, and therefore that he knows, by this argument, that an external world exists. Few people inclined to sceptical doubts have found Moore's method of argument convincing. But he defends his argument on the grounds that sceptical arguments appeal to 'philosophical intuitions' that we have less reason to accept than we have to accept common sense claims that they supposedly refute. This 'Here is one hand' argument deeply influenced Ludwig Wittgenstein, who spent his last weeks working out a new approach to Moore's argument in remarks published posthumously in *On Certainty* (1969).

Bertrand Russell (1872–1970)

Russell inherited the mantle of liberalism from John Stuart Mill whom he excelled at least in the scale and scope of his works. Yet he began his philosophical career not as a liberal philosopher but as a Hegelian idealist, having been influenced by Cambridge idealists such as McTaggart. Under the influence of G.E. Moore, he repudiated idealism and they together developed analytical philosophy which combines empirical realism with the logical analysis of concepts. Such an analysis reduces concepts and ideas to their constituents which are ultimately derived from perceptual experience.

From 1910 to 1913, Russell collaborated with A.N. Whitehead to produce the three volumes of *Principia Mathematica*. This highly technical work derives mathematics from logic by means of set theory which led to the 'new mathematics' that is now taught in our schools. However, it seems to be generally accepted that his attempt to found mathematics on logic has not been successful and indeed threatens the innovative powers of mathematics by confining it within unnatural boundaries.

The most readable and popular of Russell's philosophical works is *The Problems of Philosophy*, published in 1912. This is recommended reading for beginners in philosophy even though many of its arguments have been questioned by subsequent analytical philosophers. For the first time, philosophy was defined in terms of its 'problems' and it became the work of professional philosophers to deal with these problems, however fruitlessly. As it is easier to state the problems than work out the solution to them, a growing scepticism about philosophy's value is the inevitable result.

In that book, Russell uses a dualistic argument against idealism by distinguishing between act and object: 'Acquaintance with objects essentially consists in a relation between the mind and something other than the mind; it is this that constitutes the mind's power of knowing things.'[9] This means that reality is placed outside the mind and we are constantly interacting with it to arrive at knowledge of the contents of reality. Unfortunately, Russell doesn't develop this dualistic view in his later writings because of his commitment to logical theory. He was committed to using symbolic logic to refer to external objects. Hence his famous 'theory of descriptions' in which the existence of things is proclaimed by such formulae as '(∃x)fx' meaning 'there is an x such as x is F'.[10] The evidence for an object's existence, and the context in which such proclamations are made, are ignored in these formulae. In his paper 'On Denoting'(1905), he says that 'A logical theory may be tested by its capacity for dealing with puzzles.'[11] His theory seems to generate as many puzzles as it solves (see A.C. Grayling's *Russell* (1996), for details of these).[12]

Russell's development of logic has had the undesirable effect of making words and sentences more important than the real or unreal things and events to which they refer. This results from making truth and falsity a matter of logical form which is expressed in symbols. What matters is what we do to establish truth and falsity in a practical way, such as finding out by trial and error. Logic as ever proves nothing but the validity of its own forms of argument.

In his later work, Russell seems to have been influenced by Wittgenstein's later philosophy which downplays the importance of logic in understanding language and reference. Thus, Russell's *Human Knowledge: Its Scope and Limits* (1948) deals with how scientific knowledge is inferred from our perceptions. He anticipates the current view that we differ from animals only by degree rather than absolutely:

> In the matter of language as in other respects, there is a continuous gradation from animal behaviour to that of the most precise man of science, and from pre-linguistic noises to the polished diction of the lexicographer.[13]

All in all, Russell was a true philosopher in his constant quest for truth as he was not afraid to change his mind and follow his arguments wherever they went, regardless of criticism or fashionable opinion.

Ludwig Wittgenstein (1889–1951)

Wittgenstein owed his reputation in philosophy to his association with Bertrand Russell. It is doubtful whether he would have become as prominent if he had not been adopted by Russell as his heir in matters of logic. His *Tractatus Logico-Philosophicus* (1921) contributed to the development of logic in respect of truth tables and in its attempt to show the relationship of logic to language, mainly by means of a picture theory. But its main influence lies in its repudiation of metaphysics by a rigorous application of 'Hume's Fork'.[14] This inspired logical positivism chiefly through the group of philosophers known as 'the Vienna Circle'. Their views were propagated by A.J. Ayer in his *Language, Truth and Logic* (1936), after he had visited the Circle.

The influence of Schopenhauer is also to be found in the *Tractatus* when Wittgenstein mentions the effects of the will on the world: it can alter the limits of the world but not the facts.[15] He ends the *Tractatus* by saying: 'What we cannot speak of, we must pass over in silence.' It would be truer to say that there is always something more to be said. It is a matter of thinking of what is still to be said. Thoughts are not the same as words. But too many twentieth-century philosophers, especially postmodernist ones, followed Wittgenstein in reducing everything to words and texts, at the expense of thoughts concerning them.

In his so-called 'later philosophy', Wittgenstein went to the other extreme from his *Tractatus* views when he realised that language is much more complicated than formal logic suggests. In his *Philosophical Investigations* (1953) he implicitly recognises the importance of context in determining the meanings of words and sentences. But he deliberately avoids definite theories and conclusions in his later philosophising. He now sees philosophy as a purely descriptive exercise:

> Philosophy may in no way interfere with the actual use of language; it can in the end only describe it. For it cannot give it any foundation either. It leaves everything as it is.[16]

This is simply not true. Philosophy throughout the ages has interfered with language and invented new words and new ways of thinking about things by novel uses of language. We progress as a species by using words to think in new ways and to do things differently, thereby changing the world, for better or worse. The prevalence of Wittgensteinian thought in this matter has fostered a cultural conservatism in which people cling to concepts – the pound, their political party, football team, religion and so on – as if they were sacrosanct, changeless objects.

Wittgenstein's later philosophy is sceptical of all attempts to theorise about language and mental events. His view was that there can be no thoughts without words, and no mental events without physical or behavioral manifestations of them. There is no private language by which we express thoughts or feelings not understandable by others.[17] In other words, all subjectivity must have an objective basis. This is an extreme empiricist and materialist view that robs us of all inner life whatsoever.

Wittgenstein worked on his last book, *On Certainty* (1969), until two days before his death. It is a repetitious work and its recurring themes include the certainty of knowing that tree exists independently of our seeing it:

> I am sitting with a philosopher in the garden; he says again and again 'I know that's a tree', pointing to a tree that is near us. Someone else arrives and hears this, and I tell him: 'This fellow isn't insane. We are only doing philosophy.'[18]

Twentieth-century Oxford philosophy

Under the influence of the Cambridge philosophers, Moore, Russell and Wittgenstein, a powerful school of philosophers was established in Oxford University. It included Gilbert Ryle (1900–1976), A.J. Ayer (1910–1989), J.L. Austin (1911–1960), Stuart Hampshire (1914–2004), Peter Strawson (1919–2006), Geoffrey Warnock (1923–1995) and Bernard Williams (1929–2003). These philosophers engaged in analytical and linguistic philosophy as part of the twentieth-century attempt to professionalise philosophy. They formed a community of researchers in imitation of the scientific community. Nothing substantial has resulted from that activity except increasing scepticism about the role and usefulness of philosophy as a whole.

It is arguable that the professionalisation of philosophy around logical and linguistic analysis has turned academic philosophy into an isolated sect rather than a profession serving the needs of the public. Examining the problems of philosophy has become an end in itself. Academic philosophy is no longer a means of discovering truths that might benefit humankind, but has turned in on itself to deal with its own problems. Taking their cue from science, professional philosophers treat their colleagues' subject matter as if it were matter to be experimented upon through endless 'thought experiments' that is, speculation. Their 'modesty' forbids them from developing their arguments from first principles as the great philosophers did.

In another context, this passage might be a joke in which Wittgenstein is sending up philosophers. But he is making a serious point. In this context, he is imagining or remembering G.E. Moore sitting in his garden making such remark. In the next paragraph, Wittgenstein points out that it is insane to say that you 'know' such an obvious fact, as you really aren't informing anyone of anything. Our knowledge of the tree's existence doesn't depend on any assertion to that effect. This argument goes to the root of logic wherein existential propositions assert the existence of things without reference to context or any evidence for or against that existence. Wittgenstein had argued with Russell about this matter when he began his study of logic. Russell later facetiously accused him of claiming that the proposition: 'There is no hippopotamus in this room at present' is false. Russell says that he looked under all the tables to make sure but Wittgenstein still refused to believe it.[19] But he did not believe it because he thought that it is absurd to state something so obviously untrue. Thus, at the end of his life Wittgenstein returned to a view which he first held at the beginning of his philosophical career.

Martin Heidegger (1889–1976)

Heidegger was an existentialist philosopher who was very much within the tradition of philosophy as laid down by Hegel. His *Being and Time* (1927) is a monistic, holistic work concerned with 'being in the world' or 'Dasein' (being there), in other words, what it is to exist in the world:

Dasein is an entity which does not just occur among other entities. Rather it is ontically distinguished by the fact, in its very Being, that Being is an *issue* for it. But in that case, this is a constitutive state of Dasein's Being, and this implies that Dasein, in its Being, has a relationship towards that Being – a relationship which itself is one of Being.[20]

Such passages seem to imply that a dualistic interaction of some kind is occurring. But Heidegger will not admit this as he thinks of Dasein in absolutist terms. In fact, he inverts Hegel's Absolute by converting it into our undivided experience of external reality, namely, the Dasein into which we are thrown at birth and in which we are remain totally immersed throughout our lives whether we like it or not. This immersion in Dasein takes place in time and throughout our lives we take our time:

Everyday Dasein, the Dasein which takes time, comes across time proximally in what it encounters within-the-world as ready-to-hand and present-at-hand. The time which it has thus 'experienced' is understood within the horizon of that way of understanding Being which is the closest for Dasein; that is, it is understood as something which is itself somehow present-at-hand. How and why Dasein comes to develop the ordinary conception of time, must be clarified in terms of its state-of-Being as concerning itself with time – a state-of-Being with a temporal foundation. The ordinary conception of time owes its origin to a way in which the primordial time has been levelled off. By demonstrating that this is the source of the ordinary conception, we shall justify our earlier Interpretation of temporality as *primordial* time.[21]

Heidegger also expounded a remarkable view of truth as a disclosure or an uncovering process. He disputes the logical view of truth as agreement with or correspondce to the facts. When we say that 6 agrees with 16 minus 10 what we do is uncover the 6 which is always there to be uncovered.[22] The Dasein, or immediate experience, is the focal point of truth and not any assertions that we may make about the world. The assertion 'the hammer is too heavy' is only true in the situation in which it is found to be heavy. There is no factual situation independent of the present one to which the assertion can correspond. Our words have no single meaning distinct from the whole situation (Dasein) in which they are uncovered and used.[23] Heidegger clearly attempts to apply a coherence theory of truth to reality as a whole, though nothing more seems to have been made of that attempt.

Though Heidegger disliked being classified as an existentialist, his philosophy is concerned with many of the key elements of existentialism, such as individual choice, authenticity, 'angst' and caring for the future. And Sartre was very much influenced by Heidegger and adopted many of his terms in his works.

Jean-Paul Sartre (1905–1980)

Sartre was the quintessential existentialist who avowed himself as such, unlike others of the same school of thought who shunned such labels. He believed that for human beings 'existence precedes essence', whereas the essence of material objects precedes their existence. Mountains and houses are known for what they are merely by existing as physical objects. But our existence as physical objects precedes anything we may become as human beings. We have to work hard to bring our essences into being whereas material objects merely have to exist to become all that they are going to become. In other words, 'man makes himself', as he puts it.[24] We are not enslaved by our history (Hegel), class (Marx), our genes or our environment. Thus, Sartre was correct to equate his version of existentialism with humanism:

> Man is nothing else but what he purposes, he exists only in so far
> as he realises himself, he is therefore nothing else than the sum of
> his actions, nothing else but what his life is.[25]

Such a humanist view leads to selfish individualism if it is not tempered by contextual self-criticism. In his *Being and Nothingness* (1943), Sartre gives existentialism a Cartesian slant (as befits a Frenchman) by basing 'beingness' on conscious activity, on other words, on the *cogito* of Descartes, here meaning 'I am conscious therefore I exist'. But Sartre argues that we are always conscious of something that exists, therefore consciousness itself must be nothing since it is always conscious of something other than itself. Consciousness uses this nothingness or negation to differentiate itself from existents. In practical terms, we find out what we are by ascertaining what we are not. If I am no good at drawing, I may not regard myself as an artist.

Sartre calls the beingness of physical reality 'being-in-itself' (*être-en-soi*) whereas the conscious self is 'being-for-itself' (*être-pour-soi*).[26] If we ask what differentiates consciousness from being-in-itself, this must be nothing. Within our bodies we turn into being-in-itself to become conscious beings who can negatively differentiate ourselves from physical reality. We must continually involve ourselves in being-in-itself to stave off the nothingness that otherwise envelopes us. Unlike being-in-itself, we are not already made but must constantly make ourselves out of nothing. Our freedom therefore depends on our ability to negate being-in-itself and thus choose what we want to do rather than have our actions determined by genes, environment, or outside pressures.

An important concept for Sartre is that of 'bad faith' (*mauvaise foi*). This is also known by existentialists as 'inauthenticity' and basically means not being true to oneself. It involves negating oneself by lying to oneself. We are no longer free and become subject to the determination of being-in-itself. His famous example is that of the waiter in a café who moves too quickly and is too automatic in his movements. He seems to be acting out a game and not being himself at all.[27] Thus, Sartre is pinpointing the dehumanising effects of the jobs and professions into which we subsume our personalities and lose touch with our authentic being.

A further dimension of being involves our going beyond our own bodies and to discover 'being-for-others' (*être-pour-autrui*).[28] It may be said that Sartre develops Hegel's concern with the 'Other' in a contextual manner. By thinking ourselves into other contexts beyond our immediate selfish desires and needs, we can appreciate other points of view, other people's concerns, and ultimately the plight of the whole human race. Religion does this to excess when it compels us to enter absolutely into the context of God or some prophet or other, to the point of losing ourselves altogether.

Sartre has been criticised for making too much of our ability to make ourselves out of nothing. Much research now shows the extensive effect of our genes and environment on the formation of our personalities. However, he provides a useful vocabulary which helps us to account for our being more than just physical, material beings.

Karl Popper (1902–1994)

> Science is most significant as one of the greatest spiritual adventures that man has yet known.[29]

Sir Karl Raimund Popper dominated the twentieth century as a philosopher of science and champion of the 'Open Society', a phrase he coined and popularised. He is famed for his theory of scientific method known as 'falsification theory' in *The Logic of Scientific Discovery* (1959). Popper disputed that scientific theories are verified by observation or experiment. Such theories are held until they are falsified by experiments or better theories. Falsification theory states that unless a body of knowledge is falsifiable or refutable in some specific way, it cannot be scientific. If a theory purports to explain everything, then there is no way that it can be falsified and therefore it is dogmatic rather than scientific. On that basis, he famously refuted the claims of Marxism to be scientific.

In his later *Conjectures and Refutations* (1972) Popper amended his falsification theory to a contrast between conjectures and refutations. Unless our conjectures are refutable they are likely to be dogmatic, fixed and held with religious fervour instead of scientific detachment. But his theory defines science too narrowly. Even if a scientific theory is falsified, scientists will not readily give it up. Even Einstein admitted that any contrary experimental evidence would not have threatened his theory of relativity as it made too much sense in its own right.[30]

Popper states very appositely that 'Philosophers are as free as others to use any method in searching for truth. *There is no method peculiar to philosophy.*'[31] Perhaps the same may be said of scientists and science, but Popper is dogmatically committed to the falsification theory. This is ironic considering the extent to which he rails against dogmatism in his writings. (A notorious encounter with his equally forceful rival, Wittgenstein, is entertainingly described in *Wittgenstein's Poker*.[32]) The line of demarcation between science and non-science is not so much falsification as the 'normal science' practised by a community of scientists within their respective fields of research. Even when 'normal science' is convincingly falsified, the change may not be accepted unless the community of scientists as a whole changes its mind.

Popper is also keen to disprove the existence of induction as a description of scientific method. Induction assumes that theories are arrived at by making generalisations from observations. He argues that we arrive at theories by a number of creative, psychological processes that are not logical.[33] However, he has focused on theoretical sciences such as physics and chemistry and overlooked such observational sciences such as biology, zoology and anthropology which may well involve observations followed by theories based on these observations. Darwin made copious observations on the Galapagos Islands from which he made generalisations leading to his theory of evolution.

Popper also challenged some of the ruling orthodoxies of philosophy: logical positivism, Marxism, determinism and linguistic philosophy. In particular, he argued against over-reliance on the definitions of words. Definitions don't add to our knowledge of facts.[34] We should concentrate on arriving at true theories rather than on words and their meanings and definitions.[35] Being a nominalist, he also believed that words themselves are theory-laden and should be alterable in relation to empirical experience. This attack on what he called 'essentialism' disputes the legacy of Aristotelian logic, though Popper himself never worked out fully his revolutionary views.

Through his ideas Popper promoted a critical ethos, a world in which the give and take of debate is highly esteemed. He held that we are all infinitely ignorant, that we differ only in the little bits of knowledge that we do have, and that with some co-operative effort we may get nearer to the truth. This involves our contributing to what he called 'World 3' which contains all our objective knowledge.[36] 'World 3' obviously includes the World Wide Web to which we can all contribute and take part in. It involves interaction with both the 'World 1' of physical reality and the 'World 2' consisting of our subjective experiences.[37] This supports a theory of dualistic interaction as the ground of epistemology.

In *The Open Society and Its Enemies* (1945) and *The Poverty of Historicism* (1957), Popper developed a critique of historicism and a defence of the 'Open Society' and liberal democracy. Historicism is the theory that history develops inexorably and necessarily according to knowable general laws towards a determinate end. This Marxist view is derived from Hegel's emphasis on the abstract role of history on human affairs. Popper argued that historicism underpins most forms of authoritarianism and totalitarianism. It is founded upon mistaken assumptions regarding the nature of scientific law and prediction. He conceded that the growth of human knowledge is a causal factor in the evolution of human history, but 'no society can predict, scientifically, its own future states of knowledge'.[38] Therefore there can be no predictive science of human history.

Popper draws attention to the paradoxes of freedom, tolerance and democracy. The paradox of tolerance tells us what to do about excessive multiculturalism:

> Unlimited tolerance must lead to the disappearance of tolerance. If we extend unlimited tolerance even to those who are intolerant, if we are not prepared to defend a tolerant society against the onslaught of the intolerant, then the tolerant will be destroyed and tolerance with them . . . I do not imply that we should always suppress the utterance of intolerant philosophies; as long as we can counter them by rational argument and keep them in check by public opinion, suppression would certainly be most unwise. But we should claim the *right* to suppress them if necessary even by force; for it may easily turn out that they are not prepared to meet us on the level of rational argument, but begin by denouncing all argument; they may forbid their followers to listen to rational argument, because it is deceptive, and teach them to answer arguments by the use of their fists or pistols.[39]

Without doubt, Popper made inestimable contributions to the philosophy of science and to political science. But overall he failed to work out his philosophy systematically and in sufficient depth to make it distinctive in itself. He failed, for instance, to work out the metaphysical implications of his attack on 'essentialism', which implied a new kind of logic no longer reliant on logical definitions. Perhaps he was not quite as great a philosopher as he could have been.

W.V.O. (Willard Van Orman) Quine (1908–2000)

Quine was perhaps the most dominant American philosopher of the latter half of the twentieth century. His commitment to formal logic was established with *Methods of Logic* (1950) and he always maintained that he was an empiricist. He believed scientific method to be 'the final arbiter of truth'[40] and that only science tells us about the real world.

But other aspects of his writings are anything but empiricist or sympathetic towards logic, as he differs greatly from other analytical philosophers such as the logical atomists (e.g.Russell) and the logical positivists. He did not believe conceptual analysis to be the chief end of philosophy. In his *Two Dogmas of*

Empiricism (1951), Quine attacked the traditional distinction between analytic and synthetic statements. His attack threatened not only some long-held doctrines of the analytic tradition but also its conception of the nature of philosophy, which has generally depended upon contrasting it with the empirical sciences.

The distinction between 'analytic' and 'synthetic' statements is as follows. Analytic statements are those true or false by virtue of the meanings of their words, such as 'All bachelors are unmarried.' Synthetic statements are true or false by virtue of facts about the world, such as 'There is a cat on the mat.' This distinction had been central to logical positivism, which relies on truths being either analytic or synthetic so that any other statements, especially metaphysical ones, are simply untrue. Like other analytic philosophers before him, Quine accepted the definition of 'analytic' as 'true in virtue of meaning alone'. Unlike them, however, he did not find the definition to be coherent. He accepted that analytic statements are those that are true by definition, but then argued that the notion of truth by definition was incoherent.

Quine's criticisms contributed to the decline of logical positivism although he remained a verificationist, to the point of invoking verificationism to undermine the analytic-synthetic distinction. Sentences are verified by reference to the system as a whole and not by reducing them to sensory data.[41] In place of the analytic/synthetic distinction, Quine proposed that a sentence gets its meaning, or verifies its truth, from its relations to the language or theoretical system to which it belongs as a whole. This 'meaning holism' implies a coherence theory of truth instead of the correspondence theory favoured by empiricists. In other words, the truth or meaning of a sentence is established by its coherence with other sentences in the language or system to which it belongs. This is instead of those sentences corresponding in some way to external realities.

Quine's commitment to formal logic and empiricism seems to have prevented him from making the giant leap towards formulating a totally new approach to logic which supersedes the definition-based logic laid down by Aristotle. Instead he saves the face of formal logic by a theory of 'ontological commitment' which asserts or 'posits' the existence of entities dogmatically.[42] Thus, Quine unintentionally contributed to twentieth-century scepticism about our reasoning powers by clinging to a defective system of logic which largely misrepresents these powers.

Richard (Mckay) Rorty (1931–2007)

Rorty was an American philosopher who began working in the analytical tradition but who later rejected it. He became a sceptic as he believed that philosophy can never be based on secure foundations. This view was expressed in his *Philosophy and the Mirror of Nature* (1979).

However, his sceptical arguments are based not on first principles, for instance, like those of Hume. They are based on the debatable views of fellow professional philosophers such as W.V.O. Quine. These views are treated as if they were 'foundational' and the last word on the matter. He is laying down foundations for saying that there are no foundations, thus begging the question to be addressed. There is no absolute basis for taking the stance that he takes; hence his scepticism is just as dogmatic as the foundational doctrines which he is attacking. He argues from an empiricist point of view that reduces our experiences to sense impressions such as pains or 'c-fibre stimulations'. Not surprisingly, he abandons the view that we get our knowledge by means of 'a special relation to a special kind of object called 'mental objects'.'[43] Yet there must be something special happening in our brains when we are enthralled by beautiful art or music. At least we know what we feel.

Rorty here follows Wittgenstein's extreme empiricism which, as we have seen, questioned the privacy of mental events. Everything inside us must be accessible from the outside, otherwise we can make no sense of it. This is the opposite from the idealist view, according to which everything is happening inside us, and external reality is to be understood from that standpoint. In simple terms, either nothing is in us or everything is in us. Obviously, these diametrically opposed views are incompatible with each other. They can't both be the whole truth of the matter. Some form of interactive dualism seems to be the only answer. We interact with our environment and build up a view of external reality in our thinking about it. But this is not Rorty's 'mirror' which exactly reflects external reality. It is a constantly fluid process which always falls short of being nothing but reality. We are constantly updating and renewing our contact with reality to stay in touch with it.

Because Rorty's scepticism is grounded in an extreme empiricist view, he shows little understanding of Hegel whom he accuses of 'idealistic system-building' which aims to embrace all forms of knowledge.[44] The fact that an idealist view is necessary to get anything worthwhile done, does not occur to him. In his later book, *Contingency, Irony, and Solidarity* (1989), he sees himself as an 'ironist' who has only contingent beliefs and desires. The 'ironist' abandons the search for absolute beliefs and desires that are grounded and 'beyond the reach of time and chance'. Nevertheless, his desires seem to be pretty idealistic and absolutist:

> Liberal ironists are people who include among these ungrounded desires their own hope that suffering will be diminished, that the humiliation of human beings by other human beings may cease.[45]

These are high ideals whose practical application requires to be worked out in great detail. The 'new vocabulary' he offers in this book may facilitate talk but not necessarily action. But being a sceptic, Rorty doesn't really want to do anything. His view of philosophy is a very narrow one of endless edification.

109

It becomes nothing but endless, pointless talk, involving 'the practical wisdom necessary to participate in a conversation'. Furthermore, he goes on to say:

> One way to see edifying philosophy *as* the love of wisdom is to see it as the attempt to prevent conversation from degenerating into inquiry, into an exchange of views. Edifying philosophers can never end philosophy, but they can help prevent it from attaining the secure path of a science.[46]

Rorty clearly thinks that the only alternative to an 'edifying philosophy' is an objective, empirical science, hidebound with absolute essences, and limited by deductive logic. His scepticism is redolent of his lack of imagination and his failure to see beyond 'normal philosophy' as laid down by professional philosophers during the twentieth century. He is so immersed in empiricism that, to him, all arguments that step outside 'normal philosophy' must be scientific and involve telling 'a coherent causal story about our interaction with the world, but not our transcendental need to underwrite our mirroring by showing how it approximates to truth'.[47] Yet his whole book is designed to show the inadmissibility of the latter quest for truth. He overlooks the possibility of devising a *metaphysical* account of how we interact with the world. As we have seen, this was attempted by the German idealists but they failed because they went in the wrong direction towards absolutist inclusion. The other direction might be more fruitful as it accounts for our place in the universe as implied by our current scientific understanding. This is role for philosophers to play because it involves conceptual and speculative thinking. Instead, all that Rorty does is open the door to postmodern philosophy which takes dogmatic scepticism to its obscure and counterproductive limits.

Jacques Derrida (1930–2004)

Derrida is perhaps the best known of all the postmodern philosophers who reacted against the rational certainties of modernism. His success is also due to the formidable range and depth of his scholarship. In his philosophy, he was primarily influenced by Hegel, Husserl and Heidegger,[48] and he follows the obscure, wordy style of these writers. In *Of Grammatology* (1967), Derrida proposes a 'science of writing' called 'grammatology',[49] but this is science in the broad, Continental sense and not the empirical, rigorous, logical sense. He introduces the word 'deconstruction' but denies that it is a method of any kind or a means of analysis or criticism. It is purportedly an 'event' which occurs when we read texts in our various ways.[50] Like Wittgenstein, Derrida denies that he is doing anything systematic or theoretical (to the extent that Wittgenstein is now thought to be 'deconstructing' ordinary language in his *Philosophical Investigations*).[51]

The failure to state what deconstruction aims to achieve means that there is no limit to what the deconstructor can find in texts, if he or she so wishes. For example, Derrida refers to writing as being commonly regarded as a 'dangerous supplement' to direct speech. He gets this phrase 'dangerous supplement' from Rousseau's reference to young men's sexual habits in the educational book, *Émile* (1762).[52] Derrida makes much of such 'supplements' in relation to Rousseau's sad life depicted in his *Confessions* (1781).[53] Rousseau regarded writing as just as unnatural compared with speech as sexual perversion is compared to heterosexual activity.[54] It is here that Derrida makes his notorious comment that 'there is nothing outside of the text' (*il n'y a pas de hors-texte*, literally 'there is no outside-text').[55] In this context, he means that our understanding of Rousseau is limited to what he tells us about himself in his *Confessions*. He is not 'present' for us to interrogate him. Derrida argues that our lives similarly consist of an endless series of 'supplements' which take us away from the 'presence' of immediate reality. There is nothing but the signs representing reality that only serve to emphasise our absence from it. Speech is no less a supplementary activity than writing since it involves using signs to refer to something other than itself.

Thus, contrary to Derrida's pleas, there is a method in his madness. Deconstruction is clearly a method as it is a way of doing things with texts. It interprets texts using notions such as *différance* and, above all, such binary oppositions as absence/presence, speech/writing, and inside/outside. *Différance* means not only 'difference' but also 'deferring' as it comes from the French verb *differer* meaning 'to defer' or 'delay'.[56] In both speech and writing, our words are 'signs' that differ from what they signify. There is a delay when we use words to refer to anything 'out there'. These notions only 'trace' language and are both present in and absent from it. Moreover, Derrida regards these words as 'non-concepts' which are embedded in our language. Unlike philosophical concepts they are not generalised from language to become independent of it. They cannot be defined logically as being this or that since they are both this and that.[57]

What is going on here? Well, deconstruction all stems from Derrida's profound scepticism about abstract thought. In particular, he is sceptical of the 'logocentric' tradition in western culture. Logocentricism is the view that our words have a definable meaning by which they refer directly to things and events. This is the basis of Aristotelian logic based on identity and noncontradiction. Derrida doubts that words can be identical to the things to which they refer. They are too fuzzy to be extracted from texts and treated logically. The term 'logocentricism' is therefore comparable with Popper's 'essentialism'. In a way, Derrida provides the metaphysics behind Popper's view but he does so from a Hegelian dialectical perspective.

Derrida also claims that deconstruction seeks 'a non-philosophical site, from which to question philosophy'. Also, 'such a non-site cannot be defined or situated by means of philosophical language'.[58] He thereby goes too far in making philosophy indistinguishable from literature as a whole. Eric Matthews, in *Twentieth Century French Philosophy* (1996), suggests that Derrida is 'expanding the field of philosophy' and using deconstruction to add 'a new weapon to the armoury of philosophical criticism'.[59] This would make sense if Derrida were doing something *in* philosophy. If he wants to be understood, he is a philosopher working out first principles in a coherent way. But if he doesn't care about understanding, he is a literary writer appealing to our feelings through language. Derrida wants it both ways. By avoiding method and theory, he is being deliberately unclear and ambiguous about what he is doing and where he is going.

What distinguishes philosophy from other literary forms are the goals towards which it is directed. It is supposed to make consistent sense of the world and achieve greater understanding of ourselves and the world. Without such goals, philosophy is no more than edifying literature, as Rorty makes clear. However, Derrida shows that an important and perennial problem facing philosophy is how thought and language can refer meaningfully to the external world. His use of binary oppositions such inside/outside and present/absent may be aimless and indiscriminate but it supports the view that an account of the dualistic interaction between subject and object is the way forward for philosophy. Such an account makes our words contingent on our intelligent and flexible use of them rather than assuming them to be accurate and necessary representations of the world, as in Aristotelian logic.

Twentieth-Century Women Philosophers

Women philosophers came to the fore during the twentieth century and many of them have made important and positive contributions to philosophy. Some of them have attracted followers, but none of them are generally regarded as being 'great' philosophers. Two of them (Ayn Rand and Iris Murdoch) have had full-length feature films made about their lives, though this may be because of their success more as novelists than as philosophers. Notable twentieth-century women philosophers include the following, arranged in order of year of birth:

L. (Lizzie) Susan Stebbing (1885-1943) was an analytical philosopher influenced by G.E. Moore. She founded the journal *Analysis* in 1933 and published successful introductory books on logic. Perhaps her most impressive book is *Philosophy and the Physicists* (1937), which shows the inadequacies of physicists' arguments in such popular writings as Arthur Eddington's *The Nature of the Physical World* (1935).

Ayn Rand (1905–1982) (born Alisa Zinov'yevna Rosenbaum) was a Russian-born American novelist and philosopher. She is best known for creating a philosophy named 'objectivism' and for writing well-received novels such as *The Fountainhead*. She was a broadly influential figure in post-Second World War America, though her work attracted both enthusiastic admiration and scathing denunciation. She made a remarkable defence of philosophy before an audience of military graduates at West Point, Florida in 1974. It was called 'Philosophy: Who Needs It?' and is in the 1982 book of the same name.[60] Her 'objectivism' is a mainly an unexceptionable realism combined with humanist sentiments concerning human ability to transform life. She characterised it as a philosophy 'for living on earth', grounded in reality and aimed at achieving knowledge about the natural world and ensuring harmonious, mutually beneficial interactions between human beings. In the feature film, *The Passion of Ayn Rand* (1999), Rand is played by Dame Helen Mirren (born Ilyena Vasilievna Mironov).

Hannah Arendt (1906–1975) regarded herself as a political theorist rather than a philosopher as she was concerned not with 'man in the singular' but with men living and inhabiting the world. Nevertheless, her works may be described as philosophical since she was concerned with philosophical notions rather than with constructing a coherent political theory. She famously coined the phrase 'the banality of evil' when reporting the trial of Nazi war criminal Adolf Eichman for *The New Yorker*. Evil is often committed by the most ordinary of people who thoughtlessly obey orders and conform uncritically to mass culture. Her most influential work is *The Human Condition* (1958) in which she distinguishes labour, work and action, and stresses the importance of the *vita activa* over the *vita contemplativa*.

Simone de Beauvoir (1908–1986) was a French author and philosopher. She wrote novels, monographs on philosophy, politics, and social issues, essays, biographies and an autobiography. In her novels she expounded existentialist themes. She is now best known for her book, *The Second Sex* (1949), which is a detailed analysis of women's oppression and a foundational work of contemporary feminism. She met Jean-Paul Sartre in 1929 and had a free but close association with him till his death in 1980.

Simone Weil (1909–1943) was a French philosopher and mystic. She suffered throughout her life from severe headaches, sinusitis and poor physical co-ordination. Her brilliance, ascetic lifestyle, introversion and eccentricity limited her ability to mix with others. Her philosophy is seemingly a holistic and dualistic one reconciling a spiritual quest of the soul to its secular setting. By combining both spirituality and politics in her writings, Weil hoped to counter modern materialism and the horrors of authoritarianism. Though Jewish by birth, she eventually adopted a mystical theology that approached Roman Catholicism.

G.E.M. Anscombe (1919–2001) (Gertrude Elizabeth Margaret Anscombe, also known as Elizabeth Anscombe) was a British analytic philosopher. She was a disciple and close friend of Ludwig Wittgenstein, who treated her as an honorary man and addressed her affectionately as 'old man'.[61] She was one of the executors of Wittgenstein's will, and she edited and translated many of his books including his *Philosophical Investigations*. She wrote widely on the subjects of mind, action, logic, language and ethics. She introduced the term 'consequentialism' into ethical debate, and her short book called *Intention* (1957) was perhaps her greatest and most influential work.

Dame (Jean) Iris Murdoch DBE (1919–1999) was a British moral philosopher and novelist. Her novels were best sellers and combined rich characterisation and compelling plotlines, usually involving ethical or sexual themes. Her philosophy is very much part of the Oxford school and her best known philosophical works are *The Sovereignty of Good* (1970) and *Metaphysics as a Guide to Morals* (1992). Her first published novel, *Under the Net* (1954), was selected in 2001 by the editorial board of the American Modern Library as one of the 100 best English language novels of the twentieth century. Her life is portrayed in the feature film *Iris* (2001) with Kate Winslet as young Iris and Dame Judy Dench playing her declining years.

Mary Midgley (born Mary Scrutton, 1919) is a British moral philosopher, who was a Senior Lecturer in Philosophy at the University of Newcastle upon Tyne. She is best known for her popular books and lectures on religion, science and ethics. She strongly opposes reductionist and scientistic philosophies and is especially worried about attempts, as she sees it, to make science function as a substitute for the humanities, a role for which she claims it is wholly inadequate. Midgley has famously sparred with Richard Dawkins over selfish genes and memes, and has also written in favour of a moral interpretation of the Gaia theory. In arguing against reductionism, Midgley suggests that there are 'many maps, many windows' on reality and that 'we need *scientific pluralism* – the recognition that there are many independent forms and sources of knowledge – rather than reductivism, the conviction that one fundamental form underlies them all and settles everything'[62]

Mary Warnock, Baroness Warnock DBE, FBA (born Helen Mary Wilson, 1924) is a British philosopher of morality, education and mind, and a writer on existentialism. She is an extremely eminent public figure in Britain having been involved in a number of committees of inquiry into matters such as education and human fertilisation. In 1949 she married Geoffrey Warnock, himself an eminent philosopher and later Vice-Chancellor of Oxford University. Her philosophical works include *Existentialism* (1970), *Imagination* (1976) and *The Intelligent Person's Guide to Ethics* (1998). Her opinion of women philosophers is as follows: 'I've never known such adversarial people as women philosophers. I certainly don't think that they're little timid creatures that can't speak up in a seminar. Far from it – they sometimes dominate the scene.'[63]

Martha Nussbaum (born Martha Craven, 1947) is an American philosopher, with a particular interest in ancient philosophy, political philosophy and ethics. She taught philosophy and classics at Harvard in the 1970s and early 1980s, before moving to Brown. Her book *The Fragility of Goodness* (1985) on ancient ethics, was particularly influential, and made her a well-known figure throughout the humanities. Her more recent book, *The Therapy of Desire* (1994), has also been well received. In September 2005 she was listed among the world's Top 100 Intellectuals by Foreign Policy.

Notes

1. Bertrand Russell (1946), *History of Western Philosophy*, London: Allen and Unwin, 1962, p. 14.
2. G.E. Moore (1899), *Mind*, Vol. VIII, no. III, pp. 176–93.
3. Bertrand Russell (1959), *My Philosophical Development*, London: Allen and Unwin, 1975, ch. 5, p. 42.
4. G.E. Moore (1903), *Principia Ethica*, Cambridge: Cambridge University Press, 1968, ch. VI, 'The Ideal', §123, p. 206; also, §132, p. 219.
5. Ibid., ch. I, §12, p. 13.
6. Ibid., ch. I, §10, p. 10.
7. Ibid., ch. III, §45, p. 74.
8. G.E. Moore (1959), *Philosophical Papers*, London: Allen and Unwin, 1970, VII 'Proof of an External World', p. 146.
9. Bertrand Russell (1912), *The Problems of Philosophy*, London: Oxford University Press, 1970, ch. 4, p. 22.
10. Bertrand Russell (1905), *Logic and Knowledge*, London: Allen and Unwin, 1988, 'On Denoting', pp. 41–2.
11. Ibid., p. 47.
12. A.C. Grayling (1996), *Russell*, Oxford: Oxford University Press, Past Masters Series, 1996, pp. 36–9. Now republished as 'A Very Short Introduction'.
13. Bertrand Russell (1948), *Human Knowledge: Its Scope and Limits*, London: Allen and Unwin, 1948, Part II, ch. I, p. 72.
14. Ludwig Wittgenstein (1921), *Tractatus Logico-Philosophicus*, trans. D.F. Pears and B.F. McGuinness, London: Routledge and Kegan Paul, 1969, § 6.53, p. 151.
15. Ibid., §6.43, p. 147.
16. Ludwig Wittgenstein (1953), *Philosophical Investigations*, Oxford: Blackwell, 1968, §124, p. 49.
17. Ibid., §§256–8, pp. 91–2; §275, p. 96, etc.
18. Ludwig Wittgenstein (1969), *On Certainty*, Oxford: Blackwell, 1984, §467, p. 61. There is a photograph extant of Wittgenstein in G.E. Moore's garden showing trees in the background.

19. Bertrand Russell (1951), 'Ludwig Wittgenstein', *Mind*, Vol. LX, p. 297.
20. Martin Heidegger (1935), *Being and Time*, Oxford: Blackwell, 1987, §12, p. 32.
21. Ibid., §405, p. 457.
22. Cf. ibid., §215–16, pp. 258–9.
23. Cf. ibid., §154–5, pp. 195–6.
24. Jean-Paul Sartre (1946), *Existentialism and Humanism (L'Existentialisme est un Humanisme)*, London: Eyre Methuen, 1977, p. 50.
25. Ibid., p. 41.
26. Jean-Paul Sartre (1943), *Being and Nothingness*, London: Methuen, 1972, Part Two, ch. 1, III, p. 90.
27. Ibid., Part One, ch. 2, p. 59.
28. Ibid., Part Three, ch. 1, pp. 221–2.
29. Karl Popper (1957), *The Poverty of Historicism*, London: Routledge and Kegan Paul, 1974, III, 19, p. 56.
30. Cf. Michael Polanyi (1958), *Personal Knowledge*, London: Routledge and Kegan Paul, 1973, pp. 9–15, esp. p. 13: 'Little attention was paid to the experiments, the evidence being set aside in the hope that it would one day turn out to be wrong.'
31. Karl Popper (1959), *The Logic of Scientific Discovery*, London: Hutchinson, 1968, Preface, p. 15.
32. David Edmonds and John Eininow (2002), *Wittgenstein's Poker*, London: Faber and Faber, 2002.
33. Karl Popper (1959), *The Logic of Scientific Discovery*, Part One, ch. 1, §3, p. 32.
34. Karl Popper (1972a), *Conjectures and Refutations*, London: Routledge and Kegan Paul, 1972, Introduction, p. 20. Also, *The Poverty of Historicism* (1957), I, 10, pp. 26–7 and elsewhere.
35. Karl Popper (1972b), *Objective Knowledge*, Oxford: Oxford University Press, 1975, ch. 8, p. 310.
36. Ibid., ch. 3, pp. 106–7 and ch. 4, pp. 153–4.
37. Ibid., ch. 4, p. 155.
38. Karl Popper (1957), *The Poverty of Historicism*, Preface, p. vii.
39. Karl Popper (1945), *The Open Society and its Enemies*, London: Routledge and Kegan Paul, 1969, Vol. I, ch. 7, note 4, p. 265.
40. W.V.O. Quine (1960), *Word and Object*, Cambridge, Massachusetts: MIT Press, 1983, §6, p. 23.
41. W.V.O. Quine (1961), 'Two Dogmas of Empiricism', in *From a Logical Point of View*, New York: Harper and Row, 1963, II, 5, p. 38.
42. Cf. W.V.O. Quine (1960), *Word and Object*, §49, p. 238.
43. Richard Rorty (1979), *Philosophy and the Mirror of Nature*, Oxford: Basil Blackwell, 1980, p. 95.
44. Ibid., p. 135.
45. Richard Rorty (1989), *Contingency, Irony, and Solidarity*, Cambridge: Cambridge University Press, 1989, Introduction, p. xv.
46. Richard Rorty (1979), *Philosophy and the Mirror of Nature*, p. 372.
47. Ibid., p. 341.
48. Richard Kearney (1984), *Dialogues with Contemporary Continental Thinkers*, Manchester: Manchester University Press, 1986, 'Dialogue with Jacques Derrida', p. 109: 'My philosophical formation owes much to the thought of Hegel, Husserl, and Heidegger.'
49. Jacques Derrida (1967), *Of Grammatology*, trans. G.C. Spivak, Baltimore: Johns Hopkins University Press, 1998, p. 4.
50. Jacques Derrida (1987), 'Letter to a Japanese Friend', in *A Derrida Reader: Between the Blinds*, ed. P. Karmuf, New York: Columbia University Press, 1991, p. 273. Understandably, Professor Izutsu was having difficulty in translating the word 'deconstruction' into Japanese. (Also in *Derrida and Différance*, ed. by D. Wood and R. Bernasconi, Evanston Illinois: Northwestern University Press, 1988, pp. 1–5.)
51. Cf. Henry Staten (1985), *Wittgenstein and Derrida*, Oxford: Blackwell, 1985, ch. 2, pp. 64–5.
52. Jean Jacques Rousseau (1762), *Émile*, trans. B. Foxley, London: Dent (Everyman's Library), 1969, Book IV, p. 299: 'if once he acquires this dangerous habit he is ruined' (*s'il connoit une fois ce dangereux supplément, il est perdu.*).
53. Jacques Derrida (1967), *Of Grammatology*, Part 2, ch. 2, p. 150.
54. Ibid., p. 149.
55. Ibid., p. 158.

56. Jacques Derrida (1972), *Margins of Philosophy*, trans. A. Bass, Brighton: Harvester Press, 1986, '*Différance*', p. 8.
57. Richard Kearney (1984), *Dialogues with Contemporary Continental Thinkers*, p. 110.
58. Ibid., p. 108.
59. Eric Matthews, *Twentieth Century French Philosophy*, Oxford: Oxford University Press, 1996, ch. 8, §3, pp. 171 and 178.
60. Ayn Rand, *Philosophy: Who Needs It?* New York: Signet, 1982.
61. Ray Monk, *Wittgenstein: The Duty of Genius*, London: Vintage, 1991, p. 498.
62. Mary Midgely, *The Myths we Live By*, London: Routledge, 2003, p. 27.
63. Mary Warnock, interview in *The Philosophers' Magazine*, Issue 7, Summer 1999.

PART 2
Philosophical Subjects

2.1 Core Subjects

The core subjects are those which form the core of most philosophy courses. They are also subject to a great deal of controversy and disagreement. For that reason the content of these subjects is not stable or systematic enough for them to be considered in any way scientific. Even foundations of logic are by any means sure or certain. It has not yet been shown that logic can represent the complexities of human reasoning with any accuracy. Whether the core subjects could ever be rendered systematic enough to be scientific is itself a subject for philosophical study. Being human means not being entirely rational or predictable Therefore, it is debatable whether philosophy can be any more or less human than we ourselves are.

Metaphysics

Metaphysics remains as ever 'the queen of sciences', since all matters of first principle are metaphysical matters. First principles are the underlying assumptions on which we base our beliefs and opinions. In metaphysics we examine these principles in a systematic way to understand ourselves, the world and our place in it. Metaphysics deals with our views concerning *why* things are as they are whereas science deals with *what* and *how* they are. This includes all questions and problems of science that are still doubtful and speculative. Where science fails us, metaphysics steps in. Thus, theology is a branch of metaphysics since it concerns speculations concerning the existence and nature of God.

Metaphysics therefore includes all the core subjects of philosophy as it is the name for the speculation involved in them. The most intractable of philosophical problems are metaphysical ones. These include what we are here for, and the mind/body and freewill/determinism problems. Materialism and idealism are types of metaphysical theory which assume respectively either the reality of material objects or the reality of ideas in the mind. There is also the problem of the reality or unreality of things that continue to exist unseen by anyone. Kant thought it was a 'scandal of philosophy' that there is no proof that things really exist in the external world. Heidegger retorted that the 'scandal of philosophy' lay in the constant attempt to establish such a proof. Our access to the external world is direct and 'ready to hand' and therefore requires no proof. Whether such a proof is necessary or possible is a metaphysical matter. It will only cease to be so when the answer is given in a systematic scientific theory which is generally accepted as being the truth of the matter.

Epistemology

Epistemology concerns the theory of knowledge – what we know and how we know it. The epistemologist usually argues against sceptics who deny that we know anything with any certainty. 'How do you know that you know?' asks the sceptic. An empiricist such as A.J. Ayer in *The Problem of Knowledge* (1956) answers that we rely on our faculties such as perception, memory and our reasoning powers to give us reliable knowledge.[1] Our knowledge should conform to what our senses inform us about the world. Such knowledge is true when we can do things successfully in applying that knowledge. A rationalist such as Kant in his *Critique of Pure Reason* (1787) emphasises our use of concepts which we impose on the world. The rationalist thinks of knowledge as a coherent whole to which each bit of knowledge must relate if it is to be true. Thus, the empiricist thinks of knowledge as corresponding to reality whereas the rationalist thinks that knowledge must cohere with other bits of established knowledge. A dynamic, dualist view attempts to reconcile these apparently incompatible views by means of interaction between correspondence and coherence. Thus, epistemology as a systematic theory of knowledge may be possible, but the real test is whether it can deal adequately with the problem of knowledge, as referred to in the next part of this book.

Ontology

The word 'ontology' comes from the Greek for 'being' and it is therefore the study of being or existence in itself. Though ontology is really a branch of metaphysics, it is commonly contrasted with epistemology because of the traditional difference between Anglo-Saxon philosophers and Continental philosophers. Since Hegel's preoccupation with being, ontology has dominated Continental philosophy and it reached its apogee in works such as Heidegger's *Being and Time* and Sartre's *Being and Nothingness*.

What is it for something to exist or not exist? What kinds of things may be said to exist? Things that exist doubtfully are said to be appearances or 'phenomena' whereas real things are 'noumena'. Philosophers differ as to whether numbers, universals or concepts may be said to exist in reality. Realists such as Plato think that all such abstractions really exist whereas physical objects are appearances. Nominalists such as Hobbes think that the existence of things depends on their being named. They are distinguished because of the words or symbols which we use to refer to them.

Logic

Logic is the study of valid arguments or how to argue one's case consistently and coherently. The object of logical argument is to be consistent and coherent in what is said. Logic provides a way of formalising arguments to show the truth or falsehood of the structure of the argument. Aristotelian logic is founded on syllogisms such as 'All men are mortal, Socrates is a man, therefore Socrates is mortal.' But this kind of reasoning depends on how words are defined and has been increasingly criticised in recent times as not representing how we really think about things.

Symbolic logic is based on the three so-called 'laws of thought':

The law of identity –	A is A	*A table is what it is*
The law of contradiction –	A can't be both B and not B	*A table can't both exist and not exist at the same time*
The law of the excluded middle –	Either A or not A is the case	*A table is either there or not there*

The law of identity leads to tautologous statements which are uninformative. A table is a table and we learn nothing more about it by that statement. But definitions such as 'bachelors are unmarried men' give us necessary connections between subject and predicate. This is the basis of what is called 'predicative logic'. We seem to contradict ourselves when we accept that bachelors are unmarried men and then point out that many 'bachelors of arts' are married men and women. We obviously have to adjust our definition to accord with such facts.

The law of the excluded middle is essential to mathematics and computer science but it may be misused in human affairs. When we say that a swan is either white or black, this logically excludes the middle possibility, for example, a grey swan. Fanatics and extremists misuse this law when they say: 'You are either for us or against us. If you are not for us, then you must be against us.' Middle-of-the-road moderation is thereby ruled out.

Both logic and mathematics do not represent the self-referential nature of human thinking as they cannot refer outside themselves without paradox. This follows, firstly, from *Russell's paradox* which shows that the concept of all concepts can be conceived both to be and not to be a concept of itself. Thus, logical or mathematical variables such as x and y cannot represent the ambiguous complexity of human thought as there is invariably more to the real world than can be encompassed consistently in them. Secondly, these limitations are confirmed by *Gödel's incompleteness theorem* whereby a mathematical proof can never be completed without sacrificing consistency, nor rendered consistent by being completely worked out.[2] As Douglas Hofstadter points out in *Gödel, Escher, Bach* (1979), these two anomalies reveal the 'strange loops' in human thinking that logicians and mathematicians have been unable to represent in their systems.[3] (Such 'strange loops' may, however, be explicable in a theory of dualistic interaction.)

Ethics

Ethics is, firstly, the study of moral behaviour or how we should or ought to behave in private and in public and, secondly, the evaluation of that behaviour whether it is good, bad or indifferent. The first is concerned with social conformity and the second with the evaluation of behaviour from a more universal point of view.

'Morality' usually refers to a system of moral principles and to the use of that system in practice. 'Ethics' is the theoretical and philosophical study of morals, morality, moral values and human conduct. However, the terms 'morality' and 'ethics' are not always clearly distinguished and they are sometimes used interchangeably, for example, 'moral values' or 'ethical values'. Indeed, the word 'ethics' seems to be displacing the word 'morals' in common usage. This is because such issues as abortion, child care, blood sports and the like, are increasingly spoken of as matters of ethics rather than morals. Generally speaking:

- ➲ **Moral actions** reflect a person's values and those of society.
- ➲ **Immoral actions** go against a person's or society's values.
- ➲ **Amoral actions** are not based on any values or social norms.

Aesthetics

Aesthetics concerns the study of art, taste and beauty. It was formerly the case that the quality of an art object depended on its significance, form, attractiveness, prominence, remarkableness, the skill and ingenuity involved and so on. But there is a tendency nowadays for the public to accept as art whatever the would-be artist puts forward as being art. Thus, it is not surprising if an artist is audacious enough to consider an unmade bed as an art object. What is surprising is the fact that the art world and the public in general should come to consider such an object as 'art'. Truly the art of the common man (or woman) has become the norm in an age when being common, ordinary and 'normal' is the norm.

There are three approaches to aesthetics which involve studying:
- ➲ (1) The concepts of aesthetics such as beauty, the sublime, representation, form and style.
- ➲ (2) Aesthetic states of minds such as judgements, responses, attitudes, experiences and emotions.
- ➲ (3) Aesthetic objects such as faces, landscapes, physical objects and whatever objects are used by artists in creating artworks.

Notes

1. A.J. Ayer (1956), *The Problem of Knowledge*, Harmondsworth: Penguin, 1964, ch. 2, (ix–x), pp. 80–83, for example.
2. Cf. Ernest Nagel and James R. Newman (1959), *Gödel's Proof*, London: Routledge and Kegan Paul, 1971.
3. Cf. Douglas R. Hofstadter (1979), *Gödel, Escher, Bach: An Eternal Golden Braid*, Harmondsworth: Penguin, 1980, pp. 15–23, for example.

2.2 Peripheral Subjects

The subjects dealt with here are the philosophies of science, psychology, politics, religion, history and literary studies. These are only peripheral to philosophy in being distinct subjects or sciences in their own right. They have philosophical problems specific to themselves but they also have metaphysical and ethical problems which apply to all of them. Other peripheral subjects include the philosophies of sociology, economics, education, law, physics, biology, mathematics and so on. All of these show how philosophy enters into all academic studies at the highest level of abstract thought and analysis.

Philosophy of science

Science grew out of philosophy but its subject matter is still open to philosophical scrutiny. Physics was known as 'natural philosophy', and departments of 'natural philosophy' persisted in universities until at least the mid twentieth century. Only when the natural sciences became professionalised and specialised during the last century, did the philosophy of science become recognised as a separate discipline. Philosophy of science examines the facts of science as arrived at by scientific theory and experiment. It asks such questions as: What is a scientific fact? What is a scientific explanation or observation? In what way do theoretical entities such as electrons exist? It is a philosophical matter to wonder how entities can be both waves and particles at the same time. This becomes a scientific matter when the relationship between these can be stated mathematically, or at least coherently enough, to be confirmed or denied by experimental means.

Philosophy of psychology

The subject matter of psychology overlaps with that of philosophy to a greater extent perhaps than any other subject. Psychology involves the study of the mind and the philosophy of mind is also a closely related philosophical subject. But psychology differs most from philosophy as an experimental, empirical science. Psychologists are routinely involved in physiological, biological and genetic research in so far as these relate to the mental and social development of the individual. Rigorous research methods may also be used in such fields as clinical, developmental, educational, and social psychology.

Political philosophy

Politics uses philosophical concepts but is distinct from philosophy because its subject matter is largely practical and empirical. The very word 'political' is a matter of philosophical dispute. It originates with the affairs of the ancient Greek *polis* (city) but now refers mainly to the practices and institutions of national and local government. However, controversy surrounds the 'politicising' of our affairs, and the rights and wrongs of 'political correctness'. The professionalisation of politicians during the twentieth century has led to a 'political science' which is centred on political behaviour. First and foremost, political philosophy is the analysis of the state and its related institutions. This leads to questions about sovereignty (the power and authority assumed by the ruler) and political obligation (the duty and submission assumed by the ruled). What is the role of the sovereign and what are the limits to its power? When does political obligation arise for sovereigns and subjects and what is its extent? Political obligation tends to be upheld on grounds either of utility or of justice.

Philosophy of religion

The philosophy of religion deals philosophically with religious subjects and problems. These include the need for faith, the existence and attributes of God, the persistence of evil in the world, the role of religious revelation, the nature of miracles, life after death, the relationship between religion and morality, and the role of mysticism in religion. The philosophical treatment of these matters is liable to be negative and dismissive when they are subjected to reason, logic, evidence, or experiment. Thus, the philosophy of religion concentrates on understanding people's need for religious faith. In that respect, the philosophy of religion is closely linked to psychology and sociology.

Philosophy of history

The philosophy of history is important in an age in which the truth and reality of historical events is increasingly cast in doubt, especially by conspiracy theorists and some popular writers of history. The word 'history' may mean (1) the events and actions that make up the human past, or (2) the accounts given of that past and the means by which they are investigated, arrived at or constructed. In the first sense, history refers to what happened as a matter of fact. In the second sense, it concerns the study and description of these happenings. The philosophy of history may therefore examine the historical process as a whole and how history unfolds in that process. But it is also a second order inquiry into the means and methods, procedures and categories used to describe the historical process. The one looks at the historical material and the other to what is made of the material by historians.

Philosophy of language

The philosophy of language includes linguistics, which theorises about the structure of language, its grammar and syntax. In the twentieth century, the philosophy of language developed substantially in two areas: (1) the structure of language with Chomsky's contribution, and (2) speech act theory.

1. Chomsky's transformational grammar

Noam Chomsky (born 1928) transformed the study of linguistics with *Syntactic Structures* (1957). He argued that we have an innate capacity for understanding the formal principles underlying the grammatical structures of language. This explains how young children, in learning to speak, are able to infer the grammatical rules underlying ordinary sentences and then generate an infinite number new sentences that they had never heard before. He distinguished two levels of structure in sentences: 'surface structures', which are the actual words and sounds used, and 'deep structures', which carry a sentence's underlying meaning. We are able to create sentences by generating the words of surface structures from deep structures according to a limited set of abstract rules that allow for unlimited variation. Chomsky called these rules 'grammatical transformations' or 'transformational rules'. He argued that these rules are basically the same in all languages and correspond to innate, genetically transmitted mental structures in human beings. His emphasis on the innateness of language led to comparisons of his views with the innateness of ideas in Cartesian philosophy.

2. Speech act theory

This theory is important because it examines what we actually do with language as compared with logic which concerns only the form of our arguments regardless of what we actually mean to say with the words used. The theory originates in the work of the Oxford philosopher J.L. Austin (1911–1960). In conversation, we usually utter words, not to say something true or false nor to describe things objectively, but to perform a speech act. We make a 'performative utterance' when we intend to make an effect on the listener by informing, persuading, exhorting them or whatever.[1] Austin distinguished the locutionary, illocutionary and perlocutionary parts of a speech act. Its locutionary aspect lies in the act of saying something meaningful, its illocutionary aspect in what is achieved when we say something, and its perlocutionary aspect in the effect on others by what we say to them. Thus, the content, manner and effect of an utterance are covered by these distinctions.[2] Speech act theory has been further developed by John Searle (born 1932) in *Speech Acts* (1969).

Philosophy of literature

This subject is also known as 'Literary Studies' and it became increasingly philosophical during the twentieth century, largely under the influence of structuralism and postmodernism, both of which emphasise the importance of textual analysis and interpretation. It involves the reasoned consideration of literary works and the issues related to them, and it includes any argumentation about literature, whether or not specific works are analysed. Its inquiries have generally fallen into three broad categories: philosophical, descriptive and evaluative. Literature is criticised in terms of what it is, what it does, and what it is worth. What is literature and how does it differ from non-literature? Though we can speak of the literature of physics, it is clearly a non-literary subject. Thus, both fiction and non-fiction writings may be regarded as literature, but the philosophy of literature is usually confined to studying works of fiction, poetry and rhetorical subjects.

Notes

1. J.L. Austin (1975), *How To Do Things With Words*, Oxford: Oxford University Press, 1980, ch. I, pp. 6–7.
2. Ibid., ch. IX, pp. 108–9.

2.3 Twentieth-Century Philosophical Movements

The following are the most prominent and best known of the western philosophical movements during the twentieth century. They show how philosophy became more professionally based as the century progressed. Philosophers wrote increasingly for each other and within whatever movement they were reared. It became impossible for any philosopher to gain prominence outwith the academic milieu. The nineteenth-century philosopher John Stuart Mill, who never went to university and never held an academic position, could not have flourished in the twentieth century without doing both.

Idealism

British Hegelian philosophy died out during the early part of the twentieth century with the deaths of its various proponents. But idealist views have been advocated in a muted and circumspect way in the works of early-twentieth-century philosophers such as A.N. Whitehead (1861–1947), R.G. Collingwood (1889–1943) and John Macmurray (1891–1976). The torch of idealism is far from being extinguished. A glimmer of it is to be found in such works as *The Self-Aware Universe* (1995), by the physicist Amit Goswani, who advocates a 'monistic idealism' as a way reconciling physics with eastern mysticism. His views lack cogency and profundity, the more so as he overlooks the works of idealist philosophers such as Hegel. A form of idealism known as 'personalism' has also featured in twentieth-century American philosophy. It was first advocated by the American philosopher of religion Borden Parker Bowne (1847–1910), and it idealised personhood rather than the absolute, thereby finding the godhead in the person.

Phenomenology

Phenomenology was formulated by the German philosopher Edmund Husserl (1859–1938). It is a method for describing and analysing the objects of consciousness in a strictly scientific way. It therefore examines the immediate phenomena or appearances as they are given in consciousness without preconceived theories or views concerning these phenomena. Sartre wrote a phenomenological study of imagination in *The Psychology of Imagination* (1940), and Merleau-Ponty's *Phenomenology of Perception* (1945) is the classic phenomenological study of perception.

Firstly, phenomenology involves phenomenological reduction, or *epoché*, which describes mental acts in a way that is free of theories and presuppositions, either about those acts themselves or about the existence of objects in the world. In contrast to the psychologist, the phenomenologist disregards the causes, consequences, and physical accompaniments of mental acts. Objects, however, do not disappear altogether in such a process, since Husserl inherited from the German philosopher of psychology Franz Brentano (1838–1917) the view that every mental act is intentional, that it is 'of' or 'about' an object. The object need not actually exist. We can believe in dragons or see pink rats whether or not such things exist in the conventional sense. The object may also be an 'irreal' one, such as a number. The objects of mental acts are therefore described only as phenomena and without assuming their existence.

Secondly, further phenomenological analysis involves the eidetic reduction, which means reflecting on a particular act (e.g. seeing a tree). The features and essence (*eidos*) of this act are imaginatively varied in terms not merely of this particular act but of any comparable one (e.g, of seeing as such). For example, any object of vision must have colour, extension, and shape. Eidetic reduction may be used to examine not only sensory perception and its objects but also mathematical objects, as well as values, moods, and desires.

Finally, we examine the process by which objects are constituted or built up in the cognition of them. Seeing a tree entails a diversity of visual experiences as the tree is seen at different times, from different angles, and at different distances, yet what is seen continues to be apprehended as a single persistent object.

Pragmatism

Though pragmatism originated in the nineteenth century it has continued to be influential throughout the twentieth century. Pragmatism is broadly the view that the value of ideas, theories and opinions lies in their usefulness, workability, and practicality. The chief proponents of pragmatism were the American philosophers Charles Sanders Peirce (1839–1914), William James (1842–1910) and John Dewey (1859–1952), and the British philosopher F.C.S. Schiller (1864–1937). It was taken to extremes by William James when he emphasised the 'cash value' of pragmatic truths. A belief need only deliver the goods to be regarded as 'true'. James could thus write: 'On pragmatic principles, if the hypothesis of God works satisfactorily, in the widest sense of the word it is "true".' The antirational implications of this statement shocked many critics, including G.E. Moore and Bertrand Russell, who saw it as an invitation to wish-fulfilment and self-deception. There are perhaps three aspects of truth which pragmatism fails to take account of. These are the truth-telling, truth-seeking and truth-assessing aspects. Pragmatism seems to confuse the latter two and overlook the importance of the first. American pragmatism is still evident today in the writings of philosophers such as Richard Rorty and Hilary Putnam.

Analytical philosophy

Analytical philosophy and its various offshoots dominated philosophy, especially in Anglo-Saxon countries, throughout the twentieth century. Basically, it uses logic to analyse meanings, concepts and ideas. But it developed progressively into logical atomism, logical positivism and linguistic analysis.

Logical atomism

Logical atomism resulted from Bertrand Russell's pre-First World War collaboration with Wittgenstein on the theory of logic. It was further developed in Wittgenstein's *Tractatus*. It is the view that sentences are composed of atoms of meaning which are themselves expressible as atomic sentences. The difficulty in pinpointing such elementary components of sentences led to both philosophers abandoning this view.

Logical positivism

Logical positivism is a moribund offshoot of analytical philosophy which also stemmed from Wittgenstein's *Tractatus*. The Vienna Circle developed this philosophy which was expounded in English by A.J. Ayer (1910–1989) in his *Language, Truth and Logic* (1936).Its heyday was the 1930s but its influence petered out during the century. It was famous for its denunciation of all metaphysical speculation as being futile and meaningless. This was an extreme application of Hume's Fork, according to which the only admissible reasoning is either logical or scientific. Everything else, including his own philosophical works, is to be cast to the flames. However, metaphysics has continued to thrive since it embodies the abstract speculation on which healthy philosophical debate depends.

Linguistic analysis

Linguistic analysis is generally the product of Wittgenstein's later philosophy in which he abandoned the logical approach and concentrated on the meaning and use of words and sentences. Linguistic analysts include ordinary language philosophers such as Gilbert Ryle (1900–1976), Peter Strawson (1919–2006) and Norman Malcolm (1911–1990). They eschewed philosophical theories in favour of a close study of how everyday language is used.

Existentialism

Existentialism was extremely fashionable during the 1950s. It is no longer an active movement but its authors continue to be read and studied. These authors include Martin Heidegger (1889–1976), Karl Jaspers (1883–1969), Jean-Paul Sartre (1905–1980), Gabriel Marcel (1889–1973) and Maurice Merleau-Ponty (1908–1961). Existentialism gets its name from its emphasis on our existence being in some sense prior to our essence. We are thrown into the world devoid of inner content and have to build ourselves up by experiencing the world as it is. Existentialism rejects epistemology and the attempt to find foundations for human knowledge. Human beings are not primarily knowers but they care, desire, manipulate, choose and act. The self emerges from our experience of other people rather than from our cognitive contact with external objects. We are not detached from the world as independent observers but 'in the world' as a participatory being. We don't just exist like sticks and stones but are open to the world and the objects in it. All this implies a kind of interactive dualism which is not made explicit by existentialist writers. Existentialism includes no particular political doctrines, but it stresses both personal responsibility and an aversion to conformity and to whatever impairs human freedom. This made it conducive to Sartre's political activism in particular.

Postmodernism

Postmodernism began as a reaction against early-twentieth-century modernist art and architecture. In philosophy, it is a reaction against modernist ideas concerning the economic progress of society, the benefits of scientific progress, the promotion of individualism, and the development of the subjective self. Modernism is blamed for such twentieth-century horrors as Auschwitz, Hiroshima and the Stalinist purges, as if postmodernism itself is not also open to authoritarian and extremist excesses. In effect, postmodernism continues the old battle between the Continental and Anglo-Saxon ways of doing philosophy. It is as rationalist and obscure as the Hegelian tradition in philosophy has always been. It is mainly concerned with the criticism and interpretation of texts and is therefore a sceptical form of philosophy. The postmodernist philosophers include (in order of birth year): Hans-Georg Gadamer (1900–2002) Jacques-Marie-Émile Lacan (1901–1981), Emmanuel Levinas (born 1906), Paul Ricoeur (1913–2005), Jean-François Lyotard (1924–1998), Michel Foucault (1926–1984), Jürgen Habermas (born 1929) and Jacques Derrida (1930–2004). Postmodernism has developed in two main areas: poststructuralism and hermeneutics.

Poststructuralism

Poststructuralism concerns those postmodern philosophers such as Derrida and Foucault who abandoned the structuralist views of the anthropologist Claude Lévi-Strauss (born1908) and the linguist Ferdinand de Saussure (1857–1913).

Poststructuralists disputed structuralist claims that there can be absolute meaning independent of all cultures. In other words, they ushered in the cultural relativism which is fashionable today.

Hermeneutics

The term 'hermeneutics' comes from Hermes who transmitted the gods' messages to mortals. He also interpreted the messages and made them intelligible for mortals. It is therefore the study of theories concerning the interpretation and understanding of texts. But the word 'text' may be extended beyond written documents to any number of objects subject to interpretation, such as experiences. However, the word 'hermeneutics' has been overshadowed somewhat by the deconstruction of texts as popularised by Derrida. Of the postmodern philosophers, Gadamer, Ricoeur and Habermas are perhaps the chief proponents of hermeneutics.

PART 3

Philosophical Problems

Philosophical Problems

The philosophical problems dealt with here are among the most prominent and intractable. They exemplify the kind of problems that arise in philosophy. They are intractable but not necessarily insoluble. Some of these problems appear to be perennial but their nature changes from generation to generation as new knowledge and attitudes put a new gloss on things. Philosophy enables us to gain insight into such problems and to understand the difficulties in arriving at solutions to them.

Reality

The problem of reality is a perennial metaphysical problem since we are inter-active creatures who relate to reality to which we both belong and do not belong at the same time. We are always in doubt at to what is or is not reality. It may be just a dream from which we will awaken possibly when we die. We may be having information pumped into our brains as in a *Matrix* feature film. Philosophers question whether we can or cannot know such things.

Firstly, there is the problem of what really exists. Not everything that exists, is real, and not everything that is real, exists. We generally think of reality as meaning external reality which is 'out there' and which is constantly conceived by us as being such. But a painting of an imaginary landscape represents something that does not exist yet the landscape looks real enough. The dinosaurs in *Jurassic Park* look very real but are only computer-generated images. There are also cultural realities which have more than just a physical existence. Football is a real enough for partisan supporters of football teams but, no matter how intense their interest, it only exists physically for them when 22 people kick a round object around a rectangular patch of ground for 90-odd minutes.

Secondly, there is the problem of distinguishing between appearance and reality, though the contrast between these is by no means peculiar to metaphysics. In everyday life we distinguish between the real size of the sun and its apparent size, or again between the real colour of an object (when seen in standard conditions) and its apparent colour (non-standard conditions). A cloud appears to consist of some white, fleecy substance, although in reality it is a concentration of drops of water. In general, people are often (though not invariably) inclined to allow that the scientist knows the real constitution of things as opposed to the surface aspects with which ordinary folk are familiar. It will not suffice to define metaphysics as knowledge of reality as opposed to appearance; scientists, too, claim to know reality as opposed to appearance, and there is a general tendency on the part of empiricist philosophers to concede their claim.

But the problem of reality only arises when we treat it as a fixed notion to be analysed *a priori* in isolation from practical affairs. Reality is what we are constantly creating and recreating in our dualistic interaction with whatever is distinct from us, physically or mentally. Thus, we can only make slow but sure progress with this problem with our unending attempts to account for the nature of this dualistic interaction.

Knowledge

The problem of knowledge is also foundational in philosophy. Since Descartes, it has been mainly concerned with refuting sceptical arguments about the foundations of our knowledge. But arguably the real task for philosophy is to produce knowledge of direct use and interest to the public. This includes a better understanding of our place in the universe, what we are to do with our lives and so on. However, this task has become closely associated with idealist philosophers who take the broad view as compared with empiricist philosophers who have compartmentalised philosophy.

There is also the problem of belief and knowledge. What we believe is not knowledge unless we are very sure of our belief. Thus, knowledge is usually considered stronger than mere belief but the problem lies in showing in what ways knowledge is stronger than belief.The difference between knowing something and believing something has troubled philosophers ever since Plato dealt with it at length in dialogues such as *The Republic* and the *Theaetetus*. Knowledge seems to involve something more than simply believing. It requires an account, an explanation, theoretical understanding, evidence or whatever. Also, what we require for knowledge depends on what we are using it for. But the important point is that rigorous standards are required for reliable knowledge.

Causation

The problem of causation is a relatively recent problem in philosophy, and many philosophers have considered it to be soluble. It concerns the connection between cause and effect. We may be very confident that a noise of a passing car is caused by a car outside. But our conclusion is only based on past experience. It is not necessarily true. The noise might have come from the television, for instance.

That causal connections are potentially unreliable was brought into prominence by Hume in his *Treatise*, where he defines a cause in terms of the contiguity and resemblance of objects.[1] The relationship between cause and effect results from our associating them together because of their 'resemblance' or their association in the 'imagination'. This is basically an empiricist's view of the notion of cause. This view sees the world as containing nothing but connected or unconnected empirical objects that have their source in perception alone. Hume overlooks the extent to which these objects may be transformed by our conceiving them differently, or by putting them into a different context or theoretical viewpoint.

Thus, it is not enough to say 'that the customary conjunction of objects determines their causation'.[2] There must be concerted thought accompanying the observation of events which leads to their being conjoined in the mind. Without our having reasons to link them together, they remain isolated and singular occurrences. There is always mental activity in which the events are systematically connected in accordance with preconceived reasons, conjectures, theories, and motives.

Hume's assumption is that the conjunction of events somehow precedes or is independent of the act of observing or experiencing them. But when events are said to be causal, the conjunction of events is in fact being selected out of the complex concatenation of events which comprise any complex situation. In thinking of them as causal, the observer excludes most interconnections to focus on certain isolated ones, usually two: the cause and the effect. These may be real enough but they are not the whole story. The theories, language and culture in which they are imbedded and have their meaning and context, must also be considered to arrive a full understanding of any connection between cause and effect.

Thus, the connections that we make between cause and effect follow from our reasons and theories for making these connections and not vice versa. Inductive reasoning is important because it enables us to be more or less certain of the explanations that we have about events. The constant rising of the sun every morning can be depended upon because we know that the earth is constantly spinning round and is very unlikely to stop doing so in the near future. Our scientific knowledge assures us about the relative certainty of that event and there is very little chance of it not happening.

Induction

The problem of induction is an empiricist problem arising because of the so-called 'Hume's Law', namely, that there are no necessary connections over time. There can only be the necessary connections made in logic or the contingent connections made in inductive reasoning. But all our deductive reasonings depend on universal words based on our generalisations about the facts and events of the world. Thus, in a sense, inductive reasoning is prior to deductive reasoning. It can arrive at conclusions which are just as dependable or undependable as those of logical reasoning, as Thomas Reid long ago pointed out: 'When the induction is sufficiently copious, and carried on according to the rules of art, it forces conviction no less than demonstration itself does.'[3]

With induction, we reason from a part to a whole, from particulars to generals, or from the individual to the universal. Therefore it goes in the opposite direction from deductive reasoning. There is, therefore, no psychological reason why reasoning in one direction or the other should be more reliable than the other. It is only the reputation of Aristotle's logic which has ensured the primacy of deductive logic. So there is room in philosophy for a complete rethink about deductive and inductive reasoning and the relationship between them.

Many accounts of induction given by logicians are highly biased towards showing its weakness and unreliability. For instance, this following seems to be an example of induction: 'All observed crows are black. Therefore: All crows are black.'

In fact, this exemplifies deductive reasoning not inductive reasoning. It fails to distinguish between generalisations and universal statements. A universal statement 'all crows are black' is being deduced from another universal statement 'all observed crows are black'. The generalisation 'crows are generally black' is based not on particular observations of crows, in an empirical manner, but on a working knowledge of the species, colouring of their feathers and so on. Those logicians who are as empirically biased as Hume was, disparage inductive reasoning because they constantly think in terms of particular observations and not on the experiences and the practical and theoretical knowledge which underlies proper and reliable inductive reasoning, such as we normally expect from 'experts' in their field.

Facts and values

The distinction between fact and value is fundamental to western thinking. It encapsulates the distinction between the objective knowledge of science and mathematics, and the normative evaluations of ethics and aesthetics. Facts are usually measurable and quantifiable where as values are more qualitative. But facts are only truly objective when they are used in the context of the sciences and academic research generally. The facts we use in everyday life are invariably value-loaded. We use them all too often to suit our purposes, to convince people and even to deceive them. In other words, we value those facts which are useful or interesting to us. This leads us to base our behaviour on the facts. If such and such is the case, therefore we ought to do this or that.

Thus, the fact–value distinction comes down to a distinction between what *is* (can be discovered by science, philosophy or reason) and what *ought* to be (a judgement which can be agreed upon by consensus). This distinction was first made by Hume who pointed out that factual accounts about divine or human affairs are often followed by exhortations to do or not to do things. He questioned the reasoning that leads to an 'ought' or 'ought not' being derived from an 'is' or 'is not'.[4] Moral philosophers are still arguing as to whether such a connection can be made.[5]

The terms 'positive' and 'normative' are another way of expressing this distinction. Positive statements make the implicit claim to facts (e.g. a water molecule is made up of two hydrogen atoms and one oxygen atom), whereas normative statements make a claim to values or to norms (e.g. water ought to be protected from environmental pollution). The relationship between facts and values will always be problematic because we are constantly interacting with our facts and placing different values on them according to new facts or changing fashionable opinions.

Personal identity

John Locke was the first to draw attention to the problem of personal identity in his *Essay Concerning Human Understanding* (1700).[6] But he thought of the person or self as being some kind of immaterial substance. This was denied by Thomas Reid because it led to Hume's scepticism concerning the existence of any self apart from the immediate experiences that we undergo from second to second. Reid's view was as follows:

> A part of a person is a manifest absurdity. When a man loses his estate, his health, his strength, he is still the same person, and has lost nothing of his personality. If he has a leg or an arm cut off, he is still the same person he was before . . . My personal identity, therefore, implies the continued existence of that indivisible thing which I call myself. Whatever this self may be, it is something that thinks, and deliberates, and resolves, and acts, and suffers. I am not thought, I am not action, I am not feeling; I am something which thinks, and deliberates, and resolves, and acts, and suffers. My thoughts, and actions, and feelings, change every moment – they have no continued, but a successive existence; but that *self* or *I*, to which they belong, is permanent, and has the same relation to all the succeeding thoughts, actions and feelings, which I call mine.[7]

We might therefore say that the self is a process by which we continually identify and distinguish ourselves by means of our conscious actions. The self is recreated from microsecond to microsecond against the constant encroaching of time. But our awareness of this self is obviously due to self-consciousness, and the notion of the self originates in our being consciousness of what we are and what we are doing.

Consciousness

The problem of self-identity therefore boils down to the problem of consciousness, without which we cannot be aware of ourselves as being distinct from our environment. What consciousness is is presently a hotly debated topic with innumerable books claiming to have the solution but none apparently with success. Biologists such as Sir Francis Crick (*The Astonishing Hypothesis*, 1994) and physicists such as Roger Penrose (*Shadows of the Mind*, 1994) have been making their respective contributions to the debate, not excluding Daniel Dennett's over-optimistically entitled book, *Consciousness Explained* (1991).

Artificial intelligence (AI)

This relates to the problem of personal identity as its aim is to create intelligence artificially in a computer or a machine of some sort. This means giving a computer a consciousness and ultimately a personal identity of its own. Though so-called weak AI claims only that a system with intelligence may be built, strong AI goes further to claim that such a system could have a mind, mental states or consciousness in the same way people do. Whether machines could achieve consciousness has been put in doubt by John Searle's *Chinese Room* example.[8] A person without Chinese is locked in a room and supplied with messages in Chinese characters to which they reply. This person uses an instruction book to select the appropriate replies without knowing what the characters mean. This is analogous to how a computer works in translating texts. Thus, a computer could never have consciousness since it only has an 'instruction book, that is,, the software to create its output automatically. Whether this makes strong AI impossible is debatable.

Mind and body

The mind/body problem was made central to philosophy by Descartes' attempt to put an immaterial mind into a mechanical body without being able to say how these two 'substances' relate to each other. In the profile of Descartes it was pointed out that Cartesian dualism is a very limited form of dualism that distinguishes mind and body, the mental and the physical, and subject and object, as if there were absolute distinctions between these notions. A more realistic form of dualism is an *interactive dualism* in which we engage in a constant process of interacting with that which we conceive to be external to us. Fichte attempted to develop such a dualism by distinguishing between the self and non-self. But this led to an idealistic view in which non-contradiction is used to pinpoint what belongs to the self. The self became the absolute self and ultimately the Absolute in Hegel's philosophy.

Thus, in the idealist view, the mind is distinguished from the body by the mental activity of the self in logically positing what really exists as being independent of it. My bodily pains are independent of my experiencing them because the act of my thinking about them makes sense of what I am feeling. I contradict myself if I refuse to admit that these pains are really happening to me. But this idealistic solution to the mind/body problem makes all our reasonings about external reality subject to our reasoning powers. There is no way of linking our thoughts directly to external objects as their existence depends on our reasoning about them.

Idealistic interactions fail because they don't take account of the directness of perception in linking us to what is happening 'out there'. Just to see external reality as a stable unity before our eyes involves an immense amount of unconscious interaction with the sensory experience received via our sense organs. We habitually see external reality as being independent of us because we have built up all the skills and abilities required to see it as it really is. What we perceive is therefore directly referable to what really exists. At the other extreme from idealism is Gilbert Ryle's *The Concept of Mind* (1949) which purports to eliminate the 'ghost in the machine' altogether. There is no such thing as the mind as there is nothing but our dispositions to behave in certain ways.

Thus, the mind/body problem may never be completely resolved, because a complete account of the relationship between mind and body is not possible. Such an account can only be approached and never achieved in total. But we can be sure of the independence of external reality because of our constant efforts to account to ourselves the reality of what we conceive to be 'out there'. We are doing this all the time in our everyday lives and philosophy merely extends and enlarges this account to take an overall, holistic view of this interaction.

Freewill

Freewill is usually contrasted with determinism which says that we are entirely determined in our behaviour not only by physical causes but also by our psychological motivations. According to that view, we are not really free because everything that we do is determined by our feelings, our physical states, and ultimately our genes. We think we are free when we can do what we want to do. But we are determined in wanting to eat by our bodily needs. So we can ask whether 'we' are really in control or whether our bodies control us.

It is difficult to see how we can have freewill unless we have a personal identity which consists in having a mind distinct in some way from the body within which it operates. The very problem of freewill only arises when we fail to embrace dualism. We can prove the existence of freewill not by abstract, philosophical argument but by doing things of our own free will in the belief that we are in fact freely doing so. Thus, the constant success of our interactions with our environment is proof enough of the existence of freewill.

Moreover, we always feel that from one second to the next we can choose to do something or not to do something. Even after the event, we feel that we could have done otherwise than we actually did. It is always after the event that further analysis may, or may not, reveal that our choices have been determined by our feelings, our motivations, other people's exhortations, our genes or whatever. The more we know and understand about the influences behind our choices, the less free we appear to be.

However, though Hume was a determinist, he recognised that we are responsible as agents for our actions. Our behaviour may be totally determined, but we can still choose to behave well or badly and be responsible to others for our actions. This limited recognition of freedom is essential for the enforcement of the law, otherwise no one could be held accountable for any crime or lawbreaking since they would argue that they had no choice in the matter.

Time

Time is one of the greatest of the unsolved puzzles facing humankind. As St Augustine pointed out in 398 CE, we know what it is as long as we don't think about it.[9] The elusive nature of time follows from the fact that our knowledge of the past relies entirely on our memory. Time only seems to pass because we can remember the past as being different from the present. In that sense, time is something entirely in our minds. However, we can make no sense of events in the present unless there is a passage of time taking place independently of our thinking about it. It seems to be real in that sense. Change is either entirely in the mind, or it occurs within time and is itself a sign of passing time. Philosophers even today are divided as whether time is real or illusory.

However, there is a scientific as well as a philosophical approach to solving the problem of time. The solution may depend on a detailed reconciliation between these two approaches.

The philosophical approach to time

This has spawned two incompatible theories concerning whether time is real or unreal. The static theory of time argues for the unreality of time by showing its subjective, psychological nature and its dependence on our temporal language. The past, present and future tenses of verbs make us think that time passes independently of our thinking of it. The dynamic theory of time argues for the reality of time by stressing its 'becoming' nature. There is movement whereby the future becomes the present and the present becomes the past. Also, the future is open to new possibilities.

The scientific approach to time

This seeks the physical origins of time at the beginning of the universe. It also examines the thermodynamic 'arrow of time' whereby many events are not irreversible in time. When a piece of paper is burnt to ashes there is no physical way of reversing that event to recreate the paper as it was. The scientists' search for time takes them into the realms of quantum physics. Time seems to vanish at such levels and we have yet to understand how time emerges in the macroscopic level of everyday life.[10]

Truth

The problem with truth is that philosophers have tended to use one or more aspects of truth and ignore the others. These aspects include the following:

Absolute truth

Throughout history, humankind has been misled by the Platonic view of truth as being something divine, eternal and absolute. Grave inhumanities have been committed in the name of truth when it is regarded as being more important than human beings. This applies to absolute political and religious truths. When a political theory purports to explain everything, it becomes a body of absolute truths that must be implemented regardless of human cost, for instance, as in the case of the Pol Pot regime in Cambodia. When religion is based entirely on the absolute truth of Scripture, this can make divine truth more important than plain human truth.

Relative truth

The truth is relative to the circumstances in which it is stated and can never be the whole truth. This is also known as 'fallibilism' whereby every stated truth is fallible and may be updated or changed according to circumstances. It may involve 'suspension of belief' whereby we refrain from committing ourselves either to believe or not to believe something. On the other hand, when I safely cross a busy road, I can say with absolute truth that no vehicles ran me down on that occasion. Therefore, relative truth is particularly applicable to our beliefs but less applicable to events that have actually happened.[11]

Truth as reality

The truth concerns what really exists. According to Aristotle, 'truth consists in saying of that which is that it is, or of that which is not that it is not'.[12] This makes truth a matter of verbal reasoning so that it depends on our choice of words whether we are speaking the truth. But the truth is more than words in so far as it refers to something beyond the words used to refer to it. Thus, in a law-court, witnesses are sworn to tell 'the whole truth and nothing but the truth', but they may truthfully say something which turns out not to be the whole truth. For example, when a magician saws a woman in half, one witness may say: 'Yes, the woman really was sawn in half. We all saw it happening. It is a fact.'

But another witness may say: 'No, she wasn't really sawn in half. It was an illusion, though we don't know how it was done.' Thus, any number of people may say different things about what really happened. We need to do more than say what we believe to be true; we have to actively tell, seek and assess truth. We can treat truth as a process of moving towards complete disclosure of the facts rather than as an unattainable Platonic ideal. Facts are events, acts, ideas, notions or theories which are taken out of context so that they can be assessed in a wider context concerning their truth or falsity. We can get at the facts by truth-telling, truth-seeking and truth-assessing:

> **Truth-telling** is the ethical aspect of truth as it concerns sincerity, honesty and trustworthiness. It is also the most important aspect. If everyone lies or lacks sincerity, trust and honesty disappear. We tell the truth when we say what we mean and what is really the case. Business, scientific research and the very fabric of society depend on such trust, so it is prerequisite to the pursuit of all other forms of truth.[13]

> **Truth-seeking** is what we do in finding out things and discovering the way things really are. It involves the use of trial-and-error methods such as research studies, experiments and observations. When we look for the truth underlying the results of our researches and experiments, we arrive at theories and hypotheses by means of intuition and induction. We look for the general rules and regularities that account for what we discover to be the case. Such truth-seeking encompasses the pragmatic view of truth as well as the scientific method in general.

> **Truth-assessing** involves actively assessing our conclusions by their correspondence to reality or by validating their internal coherence by means of mathematics or logic.

By *correspondence* we relate words, sentences, hypotheses and theories to the contexts in which they function. These contexts bear the truth that we are seeking. For example, the reality of a feature film of a Dickens novel such as *Oliver Twist* might be assessed in the contexts of the novel, of our historical knowledge of the nineteenth century, of our psychological and sociological knowledge and so on. These contexts exist for us as practical tools by which we differentiate our subjective assessments from objective realities common to us all. In other words, they take us out of ourselves. Higher contexts such as life, society and the universe enable us to assess the value of our daily actions. By *coherence* we assess whether theories add up or fail to add up according to mathematical rules or whether they conform to the rules of logic. Consistency and proof are the hallmarks of such assessments. Isolated from truth-seeking, coherence takes us back into ourselves and away from objective realities, as is shown by the paradoxes mentioned in the section about logic in the previous chapter.

What are we here for?

The problem of what we are here for is perhaps the most fundamental of all philosophical problems. Every self-respecting person may have given some thought to this problem, whether or not they have arrived at settled answers to the question. Religion has traditionally given us all the answers we allegedly require to this question.

Anti-religionists would argue that ditching religion eases the problem considerably. It is then clear that we are here to enrich, nourish and replenish an otherwise empty, meaningless and purposeless universe. We light up the universe by our very presence on this planet, as we are capable of filling it with love, beauty, grace and goodness. We can be ecstatic at the privilege of living at all. Without us, the universe would have none of these things. The human race is therefore a very important species indeed.

Thus, as our knowledge and understanding of the universe advances, we can give better answers to this problem and to the problems of philosophy in general. These answers help us to make our lives more endurable and worth living. We must never give up seeking answers and we must never believe that the available answers are the only and ultimate ones. Only by constantly seeking to improve our ideas about ourselves, can we ensure that we, as a species, have a future.

In effect, each generation has the opportunity to establish for themselves the reasons why we are here. This way of forcefully stating what we are here for has always been an important function of philosophy, thus challenging and provoking the doubters to think of something better. But we remain philosophers only for long as we hold our beliefs lightly, provisionally and self-critically, with the prospect always of altering and improving them. Unlike many religious beliefs, philosophical ones are always capable of being criticised, discarded or improved. We should constantly put them to the test and be prepared to revise or abandon them when they cease to convince us wholeheartedly. We therefore interact with them impersonally rather than taking them personally. We can then make more of ourselves, thus fulfilling our dynamic potential instead of wallowing in past glories or miseries.

Concluding remarks

It is possible that the twenty-first century can better the twentieth century by means of a dynamic philosophy that is dualistic and therefore not driven to extremes. The twentieth century was dominated and almost destroyed by monistic oppositions between left and right, liberalism and conservativism, and communism and capitalism. These oppositions occur when human thinking and feeling is needlessly divided. We all have within us the propensities to go to such extremes. But we are not necessarily driven to behave that way. We can consciously adopt an attitude of mind which avoids such extremes of thought and feeling. A dynamic philosophy helps us to overcome these oppositions by recognising the equal demands of left and right thinking. Similar monistic oppositions occur in philosophy such as empiricist and rationalist, and realist and idealist views. They are overcome by moving forward and recognising the value of both points of view. A new synthesis may then emerge which is more cogent and sensible than those it leaves behind. In this way, philosophy may help the human race to progress by unblocking mental bottlenecks so that a new and a more realistic point of view may be universally adopted. In David Hume's words: 'Though a philosopher may live remote from business, the genius of philosophy, if carefully cultivated by several, must gradually diffuse itself throughout the whole society and bestow a similar correctness on every art or calling.'[14]

Notes

1. David Hume (1739), *A Treatise of Human Nature*, Book I, Part III, Sect. XIV, ed. P.H. Nidditch, Oxford: Clarendon Press, 1989, p. 170.
2. Ibid., Book I, Part III, Section XV, p. 173.
3. Thomas Reid (1774), 'A Brief Account of Aristotle's Logic' in *The Works of Thomas Reid*, ed. W. Hamilton, Edinburgh: J. Thin, 1895, p. 712a.
4. David Hume (1740), *A Treatise of Human Nature*, Book III, Part I, sect I, ed. Nidditch, pp. 469–70.
5. Cf., for example, the exchange between John Searle and R.M. Hare in *Theories of Ethics*, ed. Phillippa Foot, Oxford: Oxford University Press, 1988, chs. VII and VIII.
6. John Locke (1700 edn), *An Essay Concerning Human Understanding*, ed. P.H. Nidditch, Oxford: Clarendon Press, 1988, Book II, Ch. XXVII, Of Identity and Diversity, §7, p. 332.
7. Thomas Reid, *Essays on the Intellectual Powers of Man*, Essay III, Ch. IV, in *The Works of Thomas Reid*, ed. W. Hamilton, Edinburgh: J. Thin, 1895, p. 345a.
8. John Searle (1984), *Minds, Brains and Science*, Harmondsworth: Penguin, 1989, ch. 2, pp. 28–9.
9. Augustine, *Confessions*, trans. R.S. Pine-Coffin, Harmondsworth: Penguin, 1968, Book XI, 14, p. 264.
10. See such books as Paul Davies (1995), *About Time*, Harmondsworth: Penguin, 1995 and Peter Coveney and Roger Highfield (1990), *The Arrow of Time*, London: HarperCollins, 1991.
11. See Simon Blackburn (2005), *Truth: A Guide for the Perplexed*, London: Penguin, 2006, for a perplexing account of fallibilism and its limitations.
12. Aristotle, *Metaphysics*, Book IV, Ch. 7, 1011b26, in *The Basic Works of Aristotle*, ed. R. McKeon, New York: Random House, 1941, p. 749.
13. For more on the importance of truth as sincerity, see Bernard Williams (2002), *Truth and Truthfulness*, Princeton: Princeton University Press, 2002, ch. 5, pp. 84–5. For the importance of trust, see Francis Fukuyama (1995), *Trust*, London: Penguin, 1996.
14. David Hume (1777 edn), *An Enquiry Concerning Human Understanding*, ed. P.H. Nidditch, Oxford: Clarendon Press, 1975, p. 10.

Bibliography *of Referenced Works*

Addison, J. (1711), *The Spectator*, Vol. I, London: J.M. Dent, 1909.

Anonymous (1720), *An Account of the Fair Intellectual-Club in Edinburgh*: By a young Lady, the Secretary of the Club, Edinburgh: Printed by J. M'Euen & Co., 1720.

Aristotle, *Sophistical Refutations*, Loeb Classical Library, London: Heinemann, 1992.

Aristotle, *On Interpretation*, Loeb Classical Library, London: Heinemann, 1949.

Aristotle, *Metaphysics, The Basic Works of Aristotle*, ed. R. McKeon, New York: Random House, 1941.

Aristotle, *Ethics*, trans. J.A.K. Thomson, Harmondsworth: Penguin, 1987.

Augustine, *Confessions*, trans. R.S. Pine-Coffin, Harmondsworth: Penguin, 1968.

Austin, J.L. (1975), *How To Do Things With Words*, Oxford: Oxford University Press, 1980.

Ayer, A.J. (1956), *The Problem of Knowledge*, Harmondsworth: Penguin, 1964.

Bacon, F. (1620), Preface to *The Great Instauration*.

Bacon, F. (1620), *Novum Organum*.

Bacon, F. (1623), *De Augmentis Scientiarum*, Book 4, ch. I.

Berkeley, G. (1710), *A Treatise Concerning the Principles of Human Knowledge*, in *A Treatise Concerning Human Knowledge and Three Dialogues between Hylas and Philoneus*, London: Collins, 1972.

Berkeley, G. (1713), *Three Dialogues Between Hylas and Philonous*, in *A Treatise Concerning Human Knowledge and Three Dialogues between Hylas and Philoneus*, London: Collins, 1972.

Berlin, I. 'Two Concepts of Liberty', in *Political Philosophy*, ed. A. Quinton, Oxford: Oxford University Press, 1973.

Blackburn, S. (2001), *Does Relativism Matter?* Voltaire Lecture for the British Humanist Association at King's College London, last para. Available in full at www.humanism.org.uk, and published in part in *The New Humanist*, Spring, 2002, pp. 14–15.

Blackburn, S. (2001), *Being Good: A Short Introduction to Ethics*, Oxford: Oxford University Press, 2001.

Blackburn, S. (2005), *Truth: A Guide for the Perplexed*, London: Penguin, 2006.

Boethius, A. (*c.*524 CE), *The Consolations of Philosophy*, Harmondsworth: Penguin, 1976.

Bradley, F.H. (1897), *Appearance and Reality*, Oxford: Oxford University Press, 1969.

Burnet J. (1930), *Early Greek Philosophy*, London: A. & C. Black, 1975.

Cicero (*c.*44 BCE), *On The Good Life*, trans. Michael Grant, London: Penguin, 1971.

Coleridge, S.T. (1817), *Biographia Literaria*, London: J.M. Dent, 1975.

Copleston F. (1950), *A History of Philosophy*, New York: Image Books, 1962.

Coveney, P. and Highfield, R. (1990), *The Arrow of Time*, London: HarperCollins, 1991.

Dante Alighieri (*c.*1321), *The Divine Comedy*, trans. Dorothy L. Sayers, Harmondsworth: Penguin, 1976.

Darwin C. (1833), *The Correspondence of Charles Darwin*, Vol. I, 1821–1836, ed. Frederick Burkhardt and Sydney Smith, Cambridge: Cambridge University Press, 1985.

Davies, P. (1983), *God and the New Physics*, Harmondsworth: Penguin, 1984.

Davies, P. (1995), *About Time*, Harmondsworth: Penguin, 1995.

Davies, P. (2006), *The Goldilocks Enigma*, London: Penguin, 2007.

Dawkins, R. (2006), *The God Delusion*, London: Transworld Publishers, 2007.

Derrida, J. (1967), *Of Grammatology*, trans. G.C. Spak, Baltimore: Johns Hopkins University Press, 1998.

Derrida, J. (1972), *Margins of Philosophy*, trans. A. Bass, Brighton: Harvester Press, 1986.

Derrida, J. (1987), 'Letter to a Japanese Friend', in *A Derrida Reader: Between the Blinds*, ed. P. Karmuf, New York: Columbia University Press, 1991.

Descartes, R. (1641), *Discourse on Method* and *Meditations on the First Philosophy*, Harmondsworth: Penguin, 1968.

Dickens, C. (1839), *Nicholas Nickelby*, London: Collins, 1967.

Diogenes Laertius (*c*.300 CE), *Lives and Opinions of Eminent Philosophers*, Loeb Classical Library, London: Heinemann, 1980.

Edmonds, D. and Eininow, J. (2002), *Wittgenstein's Poker*, London: Faber and Faber, 2002.

Ferrier, J. (1854), *Institutes of Metaphysics*, Edinburgh: W. Blackwood, 1854.

Fichte, J.G. (1800), *The Vocation of Man*, trans. W. Smith, Lasalle: Open Court, 1965.

Fichte, J.G. (1802), *Science of Knowledge*, trans. P. Heath and J. Lachs, Cambridge: Cambridge University Press, 1982.

Foot, P., ed. (1967), *Theories of Ethics*, Oxford: Oxford University Press, 1988.

Frank, W.A. and Wolter, A.B. (1995), *Duns Scotus, Metaphysician*, West Lafayette, Indiana: Purdoe University Press, 1995.

Friends of Herculaneum Society website: www.herculaneum.ox.ac.uk.

Fukuyama, F. (1995), *Trust*, London: Penguin, 1996.

Gibbon, E. (1776), *The Decline and Fall of the Roman Empire*, London: J.M. Dent, 1962.

Glasgow Philosophical Society, Minutes of (1802–1820), Glasgow University Archives.

Grayling, A.C. (1996), *Russell*, Oxford: Oxford University Press, Past Masters Series, 1996.

Hegel, G.W.F. (1807), *Phenomenology of Spirit*, trans. A. Miller, Oxford: Oxford University Press, 1979.

Hegel, G.W.F. (1821), *Philosophy of Right*, trans. T.M. Knox, Oxford: Clarendon Press, 1942.

Heidegger, M. (1935), *Being and Time*, Oxford: Blackwell, 1987.

Heisenberg, W. (1962), *Physics and Philosophy*, Harmondsworth: Penguin, 2000.

Hitler, A. (1944), *Table Talk, 1941–1944*, trans. Norman Cameron and R.H. Stevens, London: Weidenfeld & Nicolson, 1953.

Hobbes, T. (1651), *Leviathan*, Harmondsworth: Penguin, 1985.

Hofstadter, D.R. (1979), *Gödel, Escher, Bach: An Eternal Golden Braid*, Harmondsworth: Penguin, 1980.

Hofstadter, D.R. (2006), *I am a Strange Loop*, New York: Basic Books, 2007.

Hofstadter, D.R. and Dennett, D.C. (1981), *Mind's I*, Harmondsworth: Penguin, 1986.

Hume, D. (1739–1740), *A Treatise of Human Nature*, ed. P.H. Nidditch, Oxford: Clarendon Press. 1989.

Hume, D. (1772 edn) [first edn 1748], *An Enquiry Concerning Human Understanding*, ed. P.H. Nidditch, Oxford: Clarendon Press, 1975.

Hume, D. (1772 edn) [first edn 1751], *An Enquiry Concerning the Principles of Morals*, ed. L.A. Selby-Bigge, Oxford: Clarendon Press, 1975.

Huizinga, J. (1924), *The Waning of the Middle Ages*, Harmondsworth: Penguin, 1955.

James, W. (1897), *The Will to Believe*, New York: Dover, 1956.

James, W. (1902), *The Varieties of Religious Experience*, London: Fontana, 1974.

James, W. (1907), *Pragmatism*, Cambridge, Massachusetts: Harvard University Press, 1975.

James, W. (1909), *The Meaning of Truth*, Cambridge, Massachusetts: Harvard University Press, 1975.

James, W. (1909), *A Pluralistic Universe*, Lincoln: University of Nebraska Press, 1996.

James, W. (1912), *Essays in Radical Empiricism*, Lincoln: University of Nebraska Press, 1996.

'Journal of the Easy Club' (1712–1715), in *Works of Allan Ramsay*, ed. A. Kinghorn and A. Law, Vol. 5, Edinburgh: W. Blackwood, 1972.

Kant, I. (1784), *Beantwortung der Frage: Was ist Aufklärung?* In *Sämtliche Werke*, Fünfte Band.

Kant, I. (1785), *The Moral Law (Groundwork of the Metaphysics of Morals)*, trans. H.J. Paton, London: Hutchinson, 1972.

Kant, I. (1787), *A Critique of Pure Reason*, trans. N. Kemp Smith, London: Macmillan, 1964.

Kearney, R. (1984), *Dialogues with Contemporary Continental Thinkers*, Manchester: Manchester University Press, 1986, 'Dialogue with Jacques Derrida'.

Kierkegaard, S. (1978) *Journals and Papers*, Vol. 5 ed. and trans. H.V. Hong and E.H. Hong, Bloomington: Indiana University Press, 1978.

Kierkegaard, S. (1846), *Concluding Unscientific Postscript*, trans. D.F. Swenson, Princeton: Princeton University Press, 1974.

Kirk, G.S. and Raven, J.E. (1957), *The Presocratic Philosophers*, Cambridge: Cambridge University Press, 1989.

Kuhn, T.S. (1970), *The Structure of Scientific Revolutions*, Chicago: University of Chicago Press, 1970.

147

Leask, N. (1998), 'Coleridge and the Idea of University', Queen's College, Cambridge website: www.queens.cam.ac.uk/Queens/Record/1998/Academic/coleridge.html

Lewis, J. (1970) *History of Philosophy*, London: English Universities Press, 1970.

Leibniz, G. (1714), *Philosophical* Writings, London: J.M. Dent, 1990.

Locke, J. (1690), *Two Treatises of Civil Government*, London: J.M. Dent (Everyman), 1970.

Locke, J. (1697), *Second Letter to Edward Stillingfleet, Bishop of Worcester*, p. 72. As in A.C. Campbell's edition of Locke's *Essay* (1891), New York: Dover, 1959.

Locke, J. (1700 edn) [first edn 1689], *An Essay Concerning Human Understanding*, ed. P.H. Nidditch, Oxford: Clarendon Press, 1988.

Luscombe, D. (1997), *Medieval Thought*, Oxford: Oxford University Press, 1997.

Macmurray, J. (1936), *Interpreting the Universe*, New York: Humanity Books, 1996.

Malthus, T.R. (1803), *An Essay on the Principle of Population*, Harmondsworth: Penguin, 1979.

Marx, K. (1845), *Theses on Feuerbach*, as quoted in *Selected Writings in Sociology and Social Philosophy*, ed. T.B. Bottomore and M. Rubel, Harmondsworth: Penguin, 1973.

Marx, K. (1848), *Manifesto of the Communist Party*, Moscow: Progress Publishers, 1973.

Marx, K. (1867), *Capital*, London: J.M. Dent, 1972.

Marx, K. (1875), *Critique of the Gotha Programme*, as quoted in *Selected Writings in Sociology and Social Philosophy*, ed. T.B. Bottomore and M. Rubel, Harmondsworth: Penguin, 1973.

Matthews, E. (1996), *Twentieth Century French Philosophy*, Oxford: Oxford University Press, 1996.

Mill, J.S. (1838), 'Bentham', in *Utilitarianism and Other Essays*, Harmondsworth: Penguin, 1987,

Mill, J.S. (1843), *A System of Logic: Ratiocinative and Inductive*, London: Longman, 1970.

Mill, J.S. (1848), *Principles of Political Economy* (Books IV and V), ed. Donald Winch, Harmondsworth: Penguin, 1970.

Mill, J.S. (1863), *Utilitarianism*, London: Collins, 1964.

Mill, J.S. (1869), 'The Subjection of Women' (in *Three Essays by J.S. Mill*), London: Oxford University Press, 1971.

Moore, G.E. (1899), *Mind*, Vol. VIII, no. III, pp. 176–93.

Moore, G.E. (1903), *Principia Ethica*, Cambridge: Cambridge University Press, 1968.

Moore, G.E. (1959), *Philosophical Papers*, London: Allen and Unwin, 1970.

Nagel, E. and Newman, J.R. (1959), *Gödel's Proof*, London: Routledge and Kegan Paul, 1971.

Nietzsche, F. (1885), *Thus Spoke Zarathustra*, trans. R.J. Hollindale, Harmondsworth: Penguin, 1967.

Nietzsche, F. (1889), *Twilight of the Idols*, Harmondsworth: Penguin, 1968.

Nietzsche, F. (1901), *The Will to Power*, trans. W. Kaufmann, New York: Vintage Books, 1968.

Pascal, B. (1662), *Pensées*, trans. A.J. Krailsheimer, Harmondsworth: Penguin, 1975.

Pierce, C.S. (1905), 'The Essentials of Pragmatism', in *Philosophical Writings of Pierce*, New York: Dover, 1955.

Plato, *Cratylus*, in *The Collected Dialogues of Plato*, ed. E. Hamilton and H. Cairns, Princeton: Princeton University Press, 1978.

Plato, *Critias*, trans. D. Lee, Harmondsworth: Penguin, 1969.

Plato, *Parmenides*, in *The Collected Dialogues of Plato*, ed. E. Hamilton and H. Cairns, Princeton: Princeton University Press, 1978.

Plato, *Phaedrus*, trans. W. Hamilton, Harmondsworth: Penguin, 1975.

Plato, *Protagoras*, in *Protagoras and Meno*, trans. W.K.C. Guthrie, Harmondsworth: Penguin, 1956.

Plato, *The Republic*, trans. D. Lee, Harmondsworth: Penguin, 1974.

Plato, *Symposium*, trans. W. Hamilton, Harmondsworth: Penguin, 1978.

Plato, *Timaeus*, trans. D. Lee, Harmondsworth: Penguin, 1969.

Polanyi, M. (1958), *Personal Knowledge*, London: Routledge and Kegan Paul, 1973.

Popper, K. (1945), *The Open Society and its Enemies*, London: Routledge and Kegan Paul, 1969.

Popper, K. (1957), *The Poverty of Historicism*, London: Routledge and Kegan Paul, 1974.

Popper, K. (1959), *The Logic of Scientific Discovery*, London: Hutchinson, 1968.

Popper, K. (1972a), *Conjectures and Refutations*, London: Routledge and Kegan Paul, 1972.

Popper, K. (1972b), *Objective Knowledge*, Oxford: Clarendon Press.

Quine, W.V.O. (1960), *Word and Object*, Cambridge, Massachusetts: MIT Press, 1983.

Quine, W.V.O. (1961), 'Two Dogmas of Empiricism', in *From a Logical Point of View*, New York: Harper and Row, 1963.

Ramsay of Ochtertyre, J. (1888), *Scotland and Scotsmen in the 18th Century*, ed. A. Allardyce, Edinburgh: W. Blackwood & Sons, 1888.

Reid, T. (1764), *An Inquiry into the Mind on the Principles of Common Sense*, in *The Works of Thomas*

Reid, ed. W. Hamilton, Edinburgh: J. Thin, 1895.

Reid, T. (1774), 'A Brief Account of Aristotle's Logic', in *The Works of Thomas Reid*, ed. W. Hamilton, Edinburgh: J. Thin, 1895.

Reid, T. (1785), *Essays on the Intellectual Powers of Man*, in *The Works of Thomas Reid*, ed. W. Hamilton, Edinburgh: J. Thin, 1895.

Rorty, R. (1979), *Philosophy and the Mirror of Nature*, Oxford: Basil Blackwell, 1980.

Rorty, R. (1989), *Contingency, Irony, and Solidarity*, Cambridge: Cambridge University Press, 1989.

Rousseau, J.-J. (1762), *Émile*, trans. B. Foxley, London: Dent (Everyman's Library), 1969.

Russell, B. (1905), *Logic and Knowledge*, London: Allen and Unwin, 1988.

Russell, B. (1912), *The Problems of Philosophy*, London: Oxford University Press, 1970.

Russell B. (1946), *History of Western Philosophy*, London: Allen and Unwin, 1962.

Russell, B. (1948), *Human Knowledge: Its Scope and Limits*, London: Allen and Unwin, 1948.

Russell, B. (1951), 'Ludwig Wittgenstein', *Mind*, Vol. LX, pp. 000–00.

Russell, B. (1959), *My Philosophical Development*, London: Allen and Unwin, 1975.

Sagan, C. (1981), *Cosmos*, London: Macdonald, 1984.

Santillana, G. de (1961), *The Origins of Scientific Thought*, New York: New American Library, 1961.

Sartre J.-P. (1943), *Being and Nothingness*, London: Methuen, 1972.

Sartre J.-P. (1946), *Existentialism and Humanism (L'Existentialisme est un Humanisme)*, London: Eyre Methuen, 1977.

Schelling, W.J. von (1797), *Ideas for a Philosophy of Nature, an Introduction to the Study of This Science*, trans. Errol E. Harris and Peter Heath, Cambridge: Cambridge University Press, 1988.

Schelling, W.J. von (1800), *System of Transcendental Idealism*, trans. Peter Heath, Charlottesville: University Press of Virginia, 1978.

Schopenhauer, A. (1859), *The World as Will and Representation*, New York: Dover, 1966.

Searle, J. (1984), *Minds, Brains and Science*, Harmondsworth: Penguin, 1989.

Sinclair, A.J. (1993), 'Thomas Reid and the Perceptual Foundations of Knowledge', unpublished MPhil thesis, University of Strathclyde Library, Thesis No. No. T 7562.

Sinclair, A.J. (1995), 'The Failure of Thomas Reid's Attack on David Hume', *British Journal for the History of Philosophy*, Vol. 3, No. 2, pp. 389–98.

Sinclair, A.J. (1998a), 'The Emergence of Philosophical Inquiry in Eighteenth Century Scotland', unpublished PhD Thesis, University of Glasgow Library, Thesis No. 11088.

Sinclair, A.J. (1998b), *The Answers Lie Within Us*, Aldershot: Ashgate, 1998.

Sinclair, A.J. (2007), 'A Humanist's Faith: Towards a Humanist Alternate to Religion,' in *Essays on the Philosophy of Humanism* available at www.essaysinhumanism.org/07sinclair.pdf

Singer, P. (1980), *Marx*, Oxford: Oxford University Press, Past Masters Series, 1983.

Smith, A. (1759), *The Theory of Moral Sentiments*, London: H.G. Bohn, 1853.

Smith, A. (1776), *An Inquiry into the Nature and Causes of the Wealth of Nations*, London: Routledge, c.1900.

Spinoza, B. (1677), *Ethics*, London: J.M. Dent, 1970.

Staten, H. (1985), *Wittgenstein and Derrida*, Oxford: Blackwell, 1985.

Tanner, M. (1994), *Nietzsche*, Oxford: Oxford University Press, Past Masters Series, 1994.

Taylor, A.E. (1926), *Plato: The Man and his Work*, London: Methuen, 1966.

Thucydides, *History of the Peloponnesian War*, Harmondsworth: Penguin, 1984.

Vico, G. (1744), *New Science*, London: Penguin, 1999.

Whitehead, A.N. (1929) , *Process and Reality*, 1929, New York: Free Press, 1978.

Williams, B. (2002), *Truth and Truthfulness*, Princeton: Princeton University Press, 2002.

Wittgenstein, L. (1921), *Tractatus Logico-Philosophicus*, trans. D.F. Pears and B.F. McGuinness, London: Routledge and Kegan Paul, 1969.

Wittgenstein, L. (1953), *Philosophical Investigations*, Oxford: Blackwell, 1968.

Wittgenstein, L. (1969), *On Certainty*, Oxford: Blackwell, 1984.

Xenophon, *Conversations of Socrates*, London: Penguin, 1990.

Index